SHORT BIKE RIDES ON CAPE COD, NANTUCKET & THE VINEYARD
FOURTH EDITION

". . . Contains . . . rides that allow you to experience, up close, this beloved landscape in all its diversity—from beaches to bogs, kettleponds to pine forests, bustling towns to vast solitary moors and sweeping ocean vistas."
— *Ideas for Better Living* magazine

"Thirty-four rides are suggested in this book with photographs and ride maps."
— *F.Y.I. Travel Tips,* Copley News Service

"More and more campers of all ages are traveling with their bicycles and taking to the road for exercise and enjoyment. *Short Bike Rides on Cape Cod, Nantucket & the Vineyard* [is] a guide to short bike rides in the Cape Cod area. . . from beaches to bogs, pine forests to bustling cities."
— *Camperways* magazine

". . . Keeps you organized and informed as you pedal through the back roads."
— *Women's Sports and Fitness* magazine

SHORT BIKE RIDES ON CAPE COD, NANTUCKET & THE VINEYARD
FOURTH EDITION

By

Edwin Mullen and Jane Griffith

An East Woods Book

The Globe Pequot Press

CHESTER, CONNECTICUT

Photos on pages 4, 16, 20, 36, and 40 by Lisabeth Huck. Photos on pages 68, 84, and 110 by Edwin Mullen. All other photos courtesy of *The Boston Globe*.

Library of Congress Cataloging-in-Publication Data

Mullen, Edwin.
    Short bike rides on Cape Cod, Nantucket & the Vineyard / by
    Edwin Mullen and Jane Griffith. – 4th ed.
        p.   cm.
    "An East Woods book."
    Rev. ed. of: Short bike rides on Cape Cod, Nantucket & the Vineyard /
    by Edwin Mullen and Jane Griffith.
        ISBN 0-8706-440-5
1. Bicycle touring – Massachusetts – Cape Cod – Guide-books.
2. Bicycle touring – Massachusetts – Nantucket Island – Guide-books.
3 Bicycle touring – Massachusetts – Martha's Vineyard – Guide-books.
4. Cape Cod (Mass.) – Description and travel – Guide-books.
5. Nantucket Island (Mass.) – Description and travel – Guide-books.
6. Martha's Vineyard (Mass.) – Description and travel – Guide-books.
I. Griffith, Jane, 1934- . II. Grifith, Jane, 1934-   Short bike rides on
Cape Cod, Nantucket & the Vineyard. III. Title. IV. Title: Short bike rides
on Cape Cod, Nantucket & the Vineyard

GV1045.5.M42C364   1991
796.6'4'0974492 – dc20   90-47204
                                                      CIP

Manufactured in the United States of America
Fourth Edition/Second Printing

About The Author

Edwin Mullen is a "Clamdigger." He qualified for that title by being born in May of 1924 on City Island, a tiny island that sits just off the coast of the Bronx borough of New York City. Drafted into the Army at age 18, he survived a brief stint as a twin-engine bomber pilot, dropping explosive devices on hapless German soldiers in Italy, which taught him that war was not the grand and glorious adventure he had been led to expect it to be.

He has been an actor, producer, purchasing agent for Yale University, and now, contentedly retired from the latter, a freelance writer.

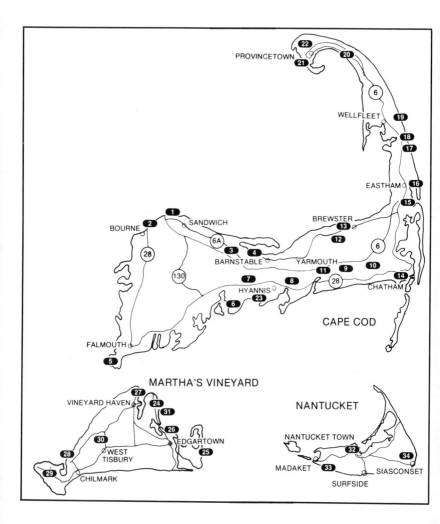

PROVINCETOWN

WELLFLEET

EASTHAM

BREWSTER

BOURNE
SANDWICH

BARNSTABLE
YARMOUTH

CHATHAM

HYANNIS

FALMOUTH

CAPE COD

MARTHA'S VINEYARD

VINEYARD HAVEN

EDGARTOWN

WEST TISBURY

CHILMARK

NANTUCKET

NANTUCKET TOWN

MADAKET

SIASCONSET

SURFSIDE

Contents

MARTHA'S VINEYARD

NANTUCKET

Introduction

These short rides provide an opportunity to explore Cape Cod and the islands in a unique and rewarding way: by bicycle on hassle-free, planned tours. The rides are from 7 to 27 miles long and range in difficulty from the flat terrain of the Cape Cod Canal to the hills of Martha's Vineyard. They can be ridden in a few hours, but to experience all the pleasures of the ride *allow at least a half day*. To ensure your enjoyment, take some precautions as outlined in the section on *Safety* and some good equipment: For picnicking and swimming, pannier bags on your rear rack and handlebar bags are indispensable. As to the bike itself, we recommend a good ten- or twelve-speed model—the best you can afford. A three-speed would be all right for the flat country rides but would take the enjoyment out of the others—and enjoyment is what it's all about.

Cape Cod

This arm of Massachusetts, site of the Pilgrims' first landfall, is about 75 miles long and has over 300 miles of coastline. Formed some ten thousand years ago by action of the retreating glacier, the Cape is a bony, sandy outcropping punctuated by bluffs, marshes, and ponds (probably created when dense ice chunks amid the debris melted away).

The Cape was settled within a couple of decades of Plymouth, and the colonists took to fishing, hunting, and haying the salt meadows. Settlers also denuded the Cape of its trees for housing, ship building, firewood, and pasture land. The cutting over, combined with the natural wash and blow dry the flora and terrain absorb from relentless waves and winds, explains the Cape's unique and fascinating appearance: rugged but right.

Cape Cod National Seashore

The Cape Cod National Seashore was created in 1961 by Act of Congress. Its 27,000 acres located in six towns are under National Parks supervision. About two-thirds of the acres are owned by the Seashore; the rest of the acreage remains in private hands or is held by the towns, but physical changes to these properties are strictly controlled.

The two Visitors' Centers, Province Lands and Salt Pond, are open seven days a week from spring until early winter. Salt Pond offers an illuminated tabletop map of the Cape, several films and dioramas illustrating the history and geology of the Cape, as well as trail guides and facilities. Province Lands Visitors' Center provides one of the Cape's most beautiful overlooks. Trail guides, exhibits, orientation talks, and rest rooms are available. Camping is not allowed in the Seashore. The dunes, flora, and fauna must remain undisturbed. Lifeguard service and public rest rooms are available at the following beaches: Coast Guard, Nauset Light, Marconi, Head of Meadow, Race Point, and Herring Cove. The Seashore extends along the Cape's entire Atlantic shore, from its southernmost point below Chatham to Provincetown. Unforgettable!

Martha's Vineyard

In 1602, wild grapes grew abundantly on the island, and in that year explorer Bartholomew Gosnold, who had a young daughter named Martha, made this vineyard her namesake.

Colonists came in 1642 to establish Edgartown, having bought the whole lash-up, unbeknownst to the Indian inhabitants who had lived there compatibly from time immemorial, for forty pounds from two gentlemen in England. The community prospered with fishing, whaling, sheep herding, dairying, and boat building, and new settlements were established. The Revolution disrupted the islanders' lives and economy, but recovery was complete by 1820 when the whaling and building booms were at their height. The triple whammy of the Gold Rush, the Civil War, and the discovery of petroleum would have resulted in a bleak future indeed had it not been for the timely burgeoning of summer religious camp meetings, which prompted a land development boom. To this day tourism is the island's principal source of income, causing the population to soar from some seven thousand year-round residents to about seventy thousand in the summer.

With that in mind, we exhort you not to bring a car here in the summer. Congestion is terrible and parking is ridiculous. From May through September—and even into October—the bike's the thing! Bring your own or rent one, and take the bus between treks. Shuttle buses run on the hour out of Vineyard Haven and on the half hour out of Edgartown via Oak Bluffs mid-May through October. Buses stop on Union Street in Vineyard Haven, at the traffic circle in Oak Bluffs, and at the courthouse in Edgartown. They run from 8:00 a.m. to 10:00 p.m. in the summer, 8:00 a.m. to 6:00 p.m. in the spring and fall.

Ferries sail from Woods Hole to Vineyard Haven year-round and to Oak Bluffs between June 16 and September 16. Boats also come from New Bedford, Falmouth, and Hyannis in the summer (June through September). Those from Falmouth and Hyannis dock only at Oak Bluffs and don't carry automobiles. After September 30 there's no service to Oak Bluffs.

If that's confusing try reading it again; if it's still confusing you can check with the Steamship Authority, (617) 540-2022 and/or Hy-Line, foot passengers only, in Hyannis at (617) 775-7185.

No camping is allowed on the beaches. There are two commercial campgrounds, one in Vineyard Haven, one in Oak Bluffs. Alcoholic beverages are sold in Oak Bluffs and Edgartown; the rest of the island is dry, but you may bring your own. Beaches open to the public include the following: in Vineyard Haven, Owen Park Beach; in Oak Bluffs, Joseph Sylvia State Beach and the Town Beach; in Edgartown, Katama (South) Beach; in Chappaquiddick, East Beach; in Chilmark, Menemsha Town Beach and Menemsha Hills; and in Gay Head, Lobsterville Beach. The Martha's Vineyard State Forest Bike Trail provides the cyclist with 14 miles of bike paths around and through this 4,000-acre pine, oak, and spruce forest. A good starting point is the Youth Hostel on the West Tisbury Road. As the forest is smack in the middle of Martha's Vineyard, however, all roads lead there! You can pick up a map of the trail anywhere on the island.

Nantucket

Nantucket, 30 miles south of Cape Cod, was created when the great ice age glacier melted away and dropped the immense load of earth and debris that shaped the island's width and length of 3 miles by 15.

Gosnold, Martha's Vineyard discoverer, also came here in 1602, but the island wasn't settled until some sixty years later when the Quakers came. The Indians were kindly disposed, which was apparently unfortunate for them: By the middle 1800s they had left or died off, and their culture vanished from Nantucket.

From 1712, when the first sperm whale was done in, until the middle 1800s, when the Fire of 1846 gutted the town and combined with the Civil War and the period's economic developments to end the bubble, Nantucket prospered, and the whaling captains built their Georgian, Federal, and Greek Revival mansions, leaving some four hundred houses here that are more than a hundred years old.

Nantucket's present economy depends largely on tourism, but commercial fishing is still a significant activity. In a unique way Nantucket depends on the past to attract people here and depends on the present to keep them coming. The island's exotic whaling history captures the imagination, but its sun, sand, flora, and moors bring one sharply into the present.

Reach Nantucket by ferry from Woods Hole, summer only ($3^{1}/_{2}$ hours) or Hyannis year-round ($2^{1}/_{2}$ hours). We urge you not to take a car here. It is a small island; you'll have a time finding a place to park on it, and the entire island is exuberantly and easily reached by bicycle. (Bring your own or rent one here.) Nantucket doesn't allow camping out or sleeping in vehicles. Public beaches are Jetties Beach, Surfside, Cisco, 'Sconset, Dionis, and Madaket.

Safety

Riding the roads of Cape Cod and the islands on a bicycle can be dangerous—if you are careless with your equipment or with yourself. Observe all Massachusetts state bicycle laws. Obey all traffic signs, lights, and other regulations. Ride with traffic, staying close to the right. Give clear hand signals. Yield to pedestrians. Ride single file. Don't ride on sidewalks in town centers. Walk your bike when going against traffic on a one-way street. Call out and slow down when approaching horses. Check your bike before beginning a trip. Make sure that all nuts are tight and that the derailleurs and brakes are working properly. No matter how long you have been riding, use a checklist before each ride. The one we use appears below.

Checklist

1. Brakes
2. Derailleurs
3. Wheel nuts
4. Tires
5. Lights
6. Reflectors and rear-view mirror
7. Bolt-cutter-proof lock
8. Tool kit
9. Rag
10. Front and rear bags
11. First aid kit
12. Head protection
13. Sunglasses
14. Insect repellent
15. Wash-N-Dry towelettes
16. Toilet paper
17. Picnic ground cloth
18. Food
19. Water bottle
20. Towel and bathing suit
21. Watch
22. Money
23. *Short Bike Rides on Cape Cod, Nantucket & The Vineyard*

See you on the road!

The Globe Pequot Press assumes no liability for accidents happening to, or injuries sustained by, readers who engage in the activities described in this book.

1. Cape Cod Canal — Sandwich

Number of miles: 17
Approximate pedaling time: 2 $1/4$ hours
Terrain: Flat
Surface: Good
Things to see: Sandwich Glass Museum, Dexter Grist Mill, Hoxie House, Heritage Plantation, Shawme Pond, glassblowers at the Pairpoint Glass factory

This lovely and varied ride starts at the Cape Cod Canal, just under the Bourne Bridge. There is a parking lot here and rest rooms (during the summer season only) maintained by the U.S. Army Corps of Engineers. Mount up and turn right onto the paved road, which runs along the canal. This road is for government vehicles (a rare sight) and bicycles only.

Follow the contour of the canal, which, in the warm months, is full of boats, large and small. The current is swift—six to seven knots at times—and often the sailboats seem to be standing still. Near the end of the canal you'll come to the NEPCO electrical power generating plant. Skirt right around it on the canal side and arrive at the Sandwich—Cape Cod Canal Marina. Go to the parking lot, turning left into it, ride straight across it, then continue bearing left, past the large Coast Guard Station and the fish company, where fresh fish is unloaded and prepared for shipment. Just past here is a gate that you go around, continuing to the very end of the canal, where you'll find a small beach. When we rode here (in the late fall), the moon was rising over Cape Cod Bay, the navigation lights were flashing, and we could see the buoys marking the entrance to the canal. A beautiful sight!

Turn around and come back along the roadway to Coast Guard Road. Turn left, past the Coast Guard Station on your right. At the stop sign turn right onto town Neck Road. Just over the railroad tracks come to a T with Tupper Road. Turn left onto Tupper. Stay on Tupper past Route 6A to the tiny center of Sandwich.

The Dexter Grist Mill was built around 1650 and still grinds cornmeal. The Hoxie House, a classic saltbox, was built in 1637,

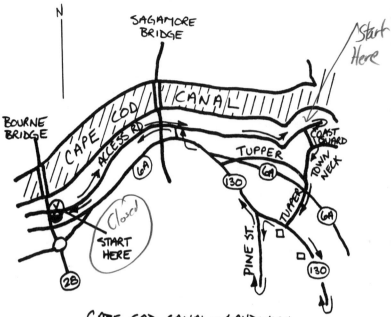

SAGAMORE
BRIDGE

Start
Here

BOURNE
BRIDGE

CANAL

CAPE COD
ACCESS RD

COAST
GUARD

TUPPER

6A

TOWN
NECK

6A

130

6A

Closed

START
HERE

TUPPER

START
HERE

PINE ST.

130

28

CAPE COD CANAL - SANDWICH

How to get there: Cross the Bourne Bridge. At the rotary turn right and then right again, downhill to the road going under the bridge. Turn right and then ~~left to the parking lot at the canal.~~ to 6A (past Sagamore Bridge), where

Turn left onto Route 130 (on the left is the Sandwich Glass Museum); just across the street, on Shawme Pond, is the Dexter Grist Mill; and up Route 130, on the shore of the pond, is the Hoxie House. The Thornton W. Burgess Museum is also here, where Burgess wrote his animal stories for children—over 170 books and 15,000 daily columns!

130 intersect 6A on right, turn left = sign
for Coast Guard. Follow CG until see corp of —

which makes it the oldest house on Cape Cod. It was acquired by the town and beautifully restored. Both the Dexter Grist Mill and the Hoxie House are open from mid-June through September. Shawme Pond is a jewel of a pond, teeming with wild geese, ducks, and swans in season. It is an artificial lake created around 1633 by the settlers who built a dam to provide water power for the mill. In April the fish ladder is packed with thousands of leaping herring (alewives) coming upstream to spawn.

After you have enjoyed all of these goodies (and if you have some time and a few dollars left), turn around and head north on 130. In about a mile you come to Pine Street. Turn left and go uphill for 0.6 mile until you come to Heritage Plantation. This is a large place, dedicated to antique America. It consists of beautiful gardens, a working windmill, a 1912 carousel, a round Shaker barn, antique automobiles, etc. Hours are 10:00 a.m. to 4:00 p.m. from May 13 to mid-October.

When you are ready to leave, return (downhill this time) to Route 130. Turn left on 130, past an old sprawling cemetery on the right, past Shawme-Crowell State Park—one of two on Cape Cod with campsites (first come, first served!). When you arrive at the junction with 6A, go left onto it; you have to turn right and then left to do so. At the fork of routes 6A and 6, bear right where the sign says ROUTE 6 AND SAGAMORE VILLAGE. Ride through Sagamore Village on the sidewalk and you'll soon see the Sagamore Bridge ahead, arching over your road as it crosses over the canal. Just before the bridge, on the right, is the Pairpoint Glass Company, a factory and store where you can watch the glassblowers practice their ancient craft: a truly rare and fascinating sight. And if you've never been in one of the ubiquitous Christmas Tree stores, there's a big one across from the Pairpoint Glass factory, up a short, steep road. These unique emporiums accept out-of-town checks—perhaps because they're a regular stop for tour buses. The Sagamore Bridge is but a few hundred feet from the glass factory. Here you turn right and make your way to the canal road, where you turn left and retrace your route the 3 1/3 miles back to the Bourne Bridge.

— Eng, l•s •n left, 3

2. Bourne

Number of miles: 18.5
Approximate pedaling time: $2^1/_4$ hours
Terrain: Varied, long flat stretches, some hills
Surface: Good
Things to see: Cape Cod Canal, Cataumet Methodist Church, Aptuxet Trading Post and Windmill, communities of Bourne, Monument Beach, Pocasset, Cataumet, and Megansett (North Falmouth)

The ride begins in the parking lot on the east side of the canal under the Bourne Bridge. There are picnic tables and rest rooms here. These facilities as well as the canal and its "Tow Path" are maintained by the Army Corps of Engineers. Mount up and go left on the Canal Service Road heading south. This is a hard-packed gravel road. After a mile, at the site of the railroad bridge, you'll reach the end of this leg. Walk your bike down the embankment and over the tracks to the parking lot. Ride through the lot and alongside the canal on Jefferson Street to the point; here, you're almost at the south end of the canal.

Now retrace the route to the parking lot, turn right on Bell Road, which may not have a street sign, and ride out to Shore Road. Turn right on Shore Road. Bear left at the fork, where there is a small traffic island. Pass Old Dam Road on the left. At a sign that points to POCASSET-2 MILES, Shore Road appears to come to a T; in fact, it jogs right and then left in front of the railroad station and a Cumberland Farms store. Continue on Shore Road. You're now in the community of Monument Beach. Upon reaching the Pocasset River, stop at the bridge and take a look at the boats. This is a colorful, picturesque scene. There's a tiny harbor, but evidently the draft is deep because there are some enormous boats moored here. This area is called Pocasset.

Continue on Shore Road past Barlow's Landing. Just before going under an overpass, you'll see a sign to the Marine Center on your right. Ride in for a look at the boats and beautiful Red Brook Harbor (if you like boats, that is). Then go under the overpass and up the hill—which is the first real hill we've encountered on this ride.

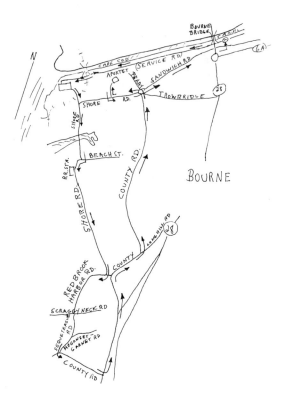

How to get there: Cross the Bourne Bridge. At the rotary turn right, then right again, downhill to the road going under the bridge. Turn right and then left to the parking lot at the canal.

Take a hairpin right on Red Brook Harbor Road. From the top of the hill, over on the right, you can see what used to be a windmill and is now a private house. Ride downhill to Parker's Boat Yard, also located on Red Brook Harbor. This community is called Cataumet. There are numerous side roads leading to the water, which you may want to explore. On this stretch you'll also see the cranberry bogs for which the Cape is justly famous. When you cross Scraggy Neck Road, Red Brook Harbor Road becomes Squeteague Harbor Road. At the intersection with Meganset Road turn right going slightly downhill on Meganset. Here, Meganset Road becomes Garnet Road, and you have just crossed into North Falmouth.

When you come to County Road, turn left. Cross the railroad tracks. Shortly, County Road will come to a T at Route 28A where there is a sign saying CATAUMET. Turn left onto 28A. You'll go up a long grade and then bear off to your left again onto another branch of County Road where there is a sign to BARNSTABLE COUNTY HOSPITAL and CATAUMET. This starts as a gently rolling road, but it becomes a fairly steep uphill as it takes you past a drive-in where you could pick up some fried clams or fish and chips before going on.

Continue on County Road at its intersection with Shore Road. Soon you'll see the Cataumet Methodist Church and cemetery. The building dates from 1765. At the fork with Long Hill Road, bear left, staying on County Road. In 2 more miles, after a couple of significant uphill grades, you'll reach a six-way intersection where there will be signs to PROVIDENCE—BOSTON—MONUMENT BEACH. Turn left on Shore Road. You'll be able to see the Aptuxet Windmill and Trading Post from Shore Road. Turn right onto Aptuxet Road and head for the windmill. Just beyond it is the Aptuxet Trading Post, originally built in 1627. There is a modest charge for the tour, which is offered from April to October 31.

After your visit come back to Shore Road, turn left, return to the intersection, and take Sandwich Road back to your starting place at the Bourne Bridge.

3. West Barnstable — Sandy Neck

Number of miles: 10.3
Approximate pedaling time: 1 hour
Terrain: Varied
Surface: Good
Things to see: Old Village Store, West Parish Meetinghouse, Sandy Neck, Great Marshes

Turn right on Meetinghouse Way (149) to start your ride. You'll promptly pass the Old Village Store. We bought excellent cheese here for a roadside snack and enjoyed poking around the store. Go uphill. At the crest you'll get a view across the Great Marshes. There is a sidewalk along this two-lane country road which you may use. In about a mile, you'll come to a fork with a road going off at forty-five degrees to your right. It is just before a large sign saying 6 WEST–BUZZARD'S BAY–BOSTON EXIT Ahead. Turn right before the sign, going past the West Parish Meetinghouse on your left. You are on Cedar Street. Pass Willow Street, Gemini Drive, and Cedarcrest Lane. The next is Maple Street, 0.7 mile from the meetinghouse; turn right. This is a gently rolling country road. Cross the railroad tracks and turn left on 6A.

Your route parallels the Great Marshes here. This extensive marsh comprises 3,000 acres. The early settlers used the "salt hay" collected here for such varied purposes as fodder, bedding, compost, thatching, and insulation. If you're ever wondering what all those little wooden boxes are that dot such areas, your curiosity can now be satisfied; they are bird houses for tree swallows attracted to the marsh to eat insects and wooden traps for horse flies (see Hugh and Heather Sadlier, *Short Walks on Cape Cod and the Vineyard,* The Globe Pequot Press).

Proceed on 6A to the fork with High Street. Bear left up High Street and enjoy another view of the Great Marshes. When you come to Howland Lane, turn right and rejoin 6A turning left.

N

SANDY NECK RD
SANDY NECK
HOWLAND RD.
HIGH ST.
WEST BARNSTABLE
GREAT MARSHES
BARNSTABLE HARBOR
MAPLE ST.
START HERE
CEDAR ST.
MEETINGHOUSE WAY (RTE 149)
MAIN ST.
6A
BARNSTABLE

How to get there: Travel east on 6A between Sandwich and Barnstable. In West Barnstable watch for a traffic light at the junction of Route 6A and Meetinghouse Way (Route 149). Turn right onto 149. Cross the railroad tracks and park on the right.

In short order, turn right on Sandy Neck Road. Ride past marshes and sand dunes to the parking lot. From there go swimming, hiking, and birding on the marked trails winding through the 6 miles of Sandy Neck dunes. The beach, being on the bayside of the Cape, is a pebbly one but nevertheless beautiful and inviting. This site is formally called Scortin Neck Beach and Nature Recreation Area. After your visit return to 6A on Sandy Neck Road. Turn left and proceed on 6A until you come to Meetinghouse Way. Turn right and return to your car in the railroad parking lot.

4. Barnstable — Cummaquid

Number of miles: 10.8
Approximate pedaling time: 1 hour
Terrain: Gently rolling
Surface: Good
Things to see: Colonial Court House, Sturgis Library, Trayser Memorial Museum

Come out of the library parking lot and head east on 6A (also called Cranberry Highway). You'll soon pass the Barnstable Comedy Club, which is an amateur theater, and the Barnstable County Court House. This building, completed in 1774, houses exhibits of flags and paintings. A film depicting Cape Cod's history is presented. Visitors are welcome on weekday afternoons from 1:30 to 4:30. Route 6A is very busy here and very narrow. There is a sidewalk on the left, and we recommend its use where there are no pedestrians.

About 2 miles from the start of the ride you'll pass the post office in the tiny community of Cummaquid. Turn left on Keveney Lane and head toward Mill Creek and Hallets' Mill Pond, going downhill. When you cross the bridge you enter a corner of Yarmouthport, and Keveney Lane becomes Mill Lane. The view of the marsh and the impressive Anthony's Cummaquid Inn is absorbing. Water Street goes off to the left shortly after crossing the bridge. Continue on Mill Lane. Return to 6A and turn right heading back to Barnstable.

If you have time, when you get to Route 6 on Mill Lane, turn left and ride a half mile to Yarmouthport to the intersection with Strawberry Lane on the right and Church Street on the left. Along this stretch are several attractions to visit briefly or to linger over. Three notable houses, which represent three hundred years of New England architecture, are open to the public: the Colonel John Thatcher House (1680), the Winslow Crocker House (1780), and the Captain Bangs Hallet House (1840). The Botanical Trail commences at the Hallet House. The houses and trail are administered lovingly by the Historical Society of Old Yarmouthport.

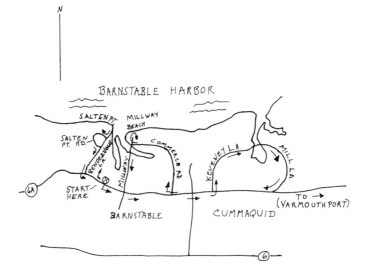

How to get there: Take 6A to Barnstable and watch for the Sturgis Library on your left shortly after passing Rendezvous Road. Park in the library's parking lot.

After enjoying Yarmouthport, turn around and head west again on Route 6A. Turn right on Commerce Road, which circles a marsh and crosses Maraspin Creek. At Mill Way, turn right for a short ride to the parking lot at Blish Point overlooking Mill Way Beach and Barnstable Harbor—dotted with islands—sheltered by Sandy Neck across the way (which you may visit on the West Barnstable ride).

Retrace the route up Mill Way past the town docks to 6A. Turn right. Ride past the Sturgis Library (where your car is parked), then turn right on Rendezvous Lane for another short jaunt to the water. On the way down to or back from the end of Rendezvous Lane (which dead ends at the water, providing a good picnic site), turn into Salten Point Road. This road makes a loop and returns you to Rendezvous Lane. It offers some stunning glimpses of the harbor, as well as a closer look at the lifestyle of some of Barnstable's burghers whose well-appointed houses and lawns are on display around this circle. Return to 6A, turn left, and head back to Sturgis Library. Built in 1644, the library's holdings include a Bible printed in 1603, as well as material relating to Cape Cod's history and genealogy.

The Trayser Memorial Museum is also located in Barnstable on 6A. It was originally a Customs House. An old jail building is on the grounds. The collection is open to the public for a modest charge Tuesday through Saturday afternoons from 1:00 to 5:00.

5. Woods Hole — Falmouth

Number of miles: 26.5
Approximate pedaling time: 3 hours
Terrain: Varied — a lot of flat areas, other definitely hilly areas
Surface: Good
Things to see: Woods Hole Oceanographic Center, Woods Hole Aquarium, views of Buzzard's Bay and Vineyard Sound, Falmouth Historical Society Museum

Ride south on 28A and bear right onto Palmer Avenue at the flashing caution light. Go down Palmer to the bottom of the hill and turn right at the fork onto a very pretty, narrow country road called Sippewisset Road. Turn right on Beccles Road for a brief loop that returns you to Sippewisset Road. When you get to the crest of the hill, you'll see what formerly was the Cape Codder Hotel, now converted into condominiums, on the bluff to the right.

Upon leaving the crest, you'll be riding mainly downhill to Woods Hole. At the first stop sign your route becomes Quisset Avenue; Oyster Pond Road will be on the left.. Turn right and go down to look at that gem of small harbors, Quisset Harbor. Come back up to the stop sign and turn right on Quisset Avenue. This downhill run will bring you abruptly into the center of Woods Hole on what is now called School Street. Eel Pond is the crowded anchorage to your right as you come into town; the buildings bordering the pond are those of the three marine research institutions: the National Marine Fisheries Service, the Marine Biological Laboratory, and the Woods Hole Oceanographic Institute. Watch for the research vessels R/V *Albatross* and R/V *Dolphin,* and visit the Woods Hole Aquarium, which is run by the National Marine Fisheries Service and is free. Quisset Avenue—now School Street—comes to a T at Water Street. Go right on Water Street to the research facilities and to see the Candle House. A unique ship's bow sticks out of the front of the building.

To continue your route, come back on Water Street to the entrance to the Steamship Authority ferry landing. (The Steamship Authority Terminal has rest rooms!) Turn right and then left into

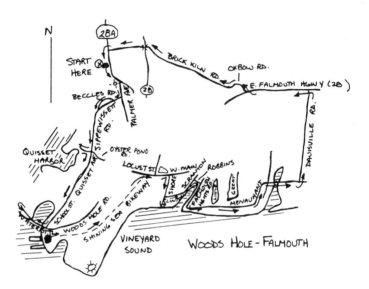

WOODS HOLE - FALMOUTH

How to get there: Head south from the Bourne Bridge on Route 28A to West Falmouth. Park south of the intersection of Route 28A and Brick Kiln Road in the parking lot of a tiny shopping center.

the large parking lot through the pedestrian entrance. Once in the parking lot, turn to your left and ride to the end of the lot, under the overpass. Here you will find the Woods Hole end of the Shining Sea Bikeway, a traffic-free ride for 3.3 miles along Vineyard Sound to downtown Falmouth.

You'll emerge from the dramatic bikeway onto Locust Street. Bear right. At the fork bear right again onto West Main Street by the Falmouth green. Watch for the elegant 1790 colonial across the green, which is the Falmouth Historical Society Museum.

At Shore Street turn right and go down to the water, see the Town Beach, and then go back up Shore two blocks to Clinton and turn right. Ride about five blocks to Scranton Avenue on the Falmouth Inner Harbor. Skirt this beautiful active harbor by going left on Scranton, right on Robbins Road at the top of the harbor, and right on Falmouth Heights Road to go down the east side. This is another site from which you can ferry to Martha's Vineyard.

Bear right at the fork onto Grand Avenue and turn sharply left as it skirts Vineyard Sound. Continue along this road, which becomes Menauhant Road, passing Little Pond and Great Pond. At the fork with Ocean Avenue (or Vineyard Street as it may be named), turn left and go inland, staying on Menauhant Road. At its intersection with Emerson (on the left), bear right, staying on Menauhant. Cross Acapesket Road, cross the bridge over Green Pond, and then turn left on Davisville Road.

Turn left at the traffic light on East Falmouth Highway, which is also Route 28. In about 0.75 mile, cross the Coonamesett River and turn right on OxBow Road. Curve around uphill and turn right, going uphill on Brick Kiln Road. Follow Brick Kiln for 3 miles to Route 28. Go under Route 28 to Route 28A and turn left to return to the shopping center parking lot.

6. Osterville — Centerville

Number of miles: 14
Approximate pedaling time: 1¹/₂ hours
Terrain: Hilly
Surface: Good
Things to see: Towns of Osterville and Centerville; East, West, and Great Bays; Crosby Yacht Yard

Begin this ride in the village of Osterville. Park your car on Main Street and head north on Main toward Falmouth. You'll pass Blossom Avenue and Emily Way, both on the right; when you come to Pond Street, turn right. Use the sidewalk on Pond and pass Tower Hill Road on the right. At the next street, Pond Street becomes Bumps River Road, which comes in from the left. Continue straight on Bumps River Road.

Soon you will come to a fork in the road, just after Old Mill Road. Depending on the time of year, the street signs may be missing, having departed the scene with some larcenous visitor, so look for a green fire hydrant on the corner and bear right, continuing on Bumps River Road. If you continued straight ahead and then curved to the left, you would find that you were on Five Corners Road. At the T intersection turn left on what is Park Avenue, though once again it may not, alas, be so marked. Ride the short distance to Henry Place. Turn right and immediately right again onto Main Street. Now you are in for a treat, as Centerville's Main Street is exceptional. There are stately old houses on both sides of the street, a handsome church, and the 1856 Country Store, which is stuffed with handmade crafts and enough gadgets to satisfy anyone.

Where Main Street intersects with South Main Street, there is a traffic light; turn right following the sign to OSTERVILLE. Proceed on South Main Street and enjoy the views of East Bay. Turn left onto East Bay Road, following it to the T intersection with Wianno Avenue. Turn left and ride to Dowes Beach. Wianno Avenue comes to a T at Seaview Avenue; turn right and follow Seaview. After passing the gatehouses, backyards, and driveways of them

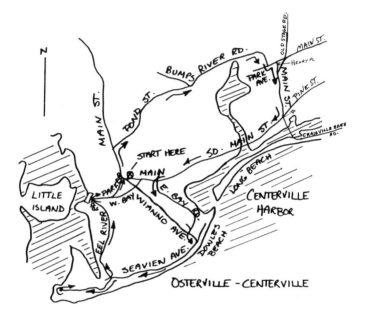

OSTERVILLE - CENTERVILLE

How to get there: From the intersection of Routes 149 and 28, head east toward Hyannis on Route 28. Take South County Road to the right. It becomes Main Street and delivers you to the center of Osterville.

that has deep pockets, you'll arrive at the end of Seaview Avenue. Here you'll be looking at a sandbar called Dead Neck, Grand Island, and West Bay.

After enjoying the scene, retrace your route to just past Eel River and turn left on Eel River Road. It will come to a T at West Bay Road. Turn left. Immediately you'll be at the Crosby Yacht Yard. Operational since 1840, this yard was the home of the Crosby Cat, the original Catboat.

Leaving Crosby's, turn left on West Bay Road and then turn left on Parker Road—which turns into Main Street—and return to the village of Osterville.

7. Hyannis

Number of miles: 13.5
Approximate pedaling time: 2 hours
Terrain: Mostly flat, a few moderate hills
Surface: Good
Things to see: Hyannis Harbor, Sunset Hill, Craigville Beach, 1856 Country Store, Kalmus Beach Park

Begin this ride from the large parking lot for the Factory Outlet Stores & Flea Market at the corner of Main Street and High School Road in Hyannis. Turn right on Main, going west (it's one way in this direction); use the sidewalk wherever possible, giving pedestrians the right of way. At Sea Street turn left and head south, passing bed and breakfast inns on both sides of the street as you head for the water. It's 1 mile to Ocean Avenue, where you bear right forty-five degrees to ride alongside the harbor and town beach for 0.5 mile to a T intersection with Hyannis Avenue. Turn left on Hyannis. Note the sign TOUR BUSES TURN RIGHT. The buses come to these short and narrow streets to show what they can of the Kennedy family compound of summer homes.

Hyannis Avenue quickly turns right almost ninety degrees and becomes Washington Avenue. Turn left at the first street, Iyanough, and immediately right onto Wachusetts Avenue. Turn left at the T intersection with Scudder, go one block, turn right onto Irving Avenue, and go up the short hill to the end of Irving. This is Sunset Hill, which used to be a public overlook where you could see the sunset and two of the Kennedy homes down on the shore. Because of tragic history of the Kennedys, the overlook is now fenced off, owned by a private golf club. There is still a view; it's just not what it was. When you are ready, go back to Scudder and turn left, riding downhill to the Y intersection with Craigville Beach Road. There's a firehouse on the right. Go left onto Craigville Beach Road, which curves left and then straightens out after it passes another Y. Keep to the left, past Strawberry Hill Road, until you reach crescent-shaped Craigville Beach, which, together with Covell and Downs beaches, forms the beaches of Craigville Harbor, a large portion of which is public and a lovely place to swim.

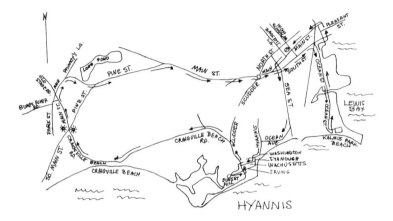

How to get there: From east or west take Route 6 or 6A to Route 132 south toward Hyannis. At the junction with Route 28 and Barnstable Road, turn right on Barnstable. If you are on Route 28, turn left if coming from the east and right if from the west. Turn right at Main Street and park in the lot at Main and High School.

To continue, follow Craigville Beach Road as it curves right, going inland, over the Centerville River to a traffic light at the intersection of Pine on the right, South Main Street on the left (and a sign reading OSTERVILLE, and your road, which goes across South Main Street and then becomes Main Street. Straight ahead is the 1856 General Store, a must stop! On this remarkable street you'll pass one stately house after another, including the Mary Lincoln house (1840), now a museum of the Centerville Historical Society.

Just past the museum, a short street, Henry Place, comes in from the left, forming the base of the triangular intersection of Main Street, Park, and Old Stage Road. Bear right, continuing on Main, which quickly comes to another Y, this time with Phinney's Lane straight ahead. Bear right again, continuing on Main as it curves to the right around the south end of Long Pond to a stop sign, where Main merges into Pine Street coming in from the right. Continue on what is now Pine Street for about 0.75 mile to a stop sign at the T intersection with West Main Street. Turn right onto West Main and use the sidewalk. In about a mile you'll come to a traffic light at Pitchers Way. Continue across on West Main for 0.5 mile to a rotary, from which you go right on Main (after Scudder). Main soon forks; bear right onto South Street. If it's getting late or you are tired, you could turn left when you get to High School Road and ride the one block to your starting place. If you're still rarin' to go, ride about seven blocks to Ocean Street, turn right, and ride down to the town park alongside Lewis Bay, where you can see lots of boat action: large ferries to the islands backing and turning, fishing trawlers, and private yachts—a cornucopia for boat watchers. And last but not least, you'll also find rest rooms and places to lock up your bike!

If you'd like a swim or a walk on a lovely beach, continue down Ocean about 0.5 mile to Kalmus Park Beach. When you are ready, return up Ocean to South Street. To avoid the heavy traffic here, turn right on South and ride the short distance to Pleasant, where you turn left and ride to Main Street; turn left and ride down to the starting place at High School Road and Main.

8. West Yarmouth — South Yarmouth

Number of miles: 14.5
Approximate pedaling time: 2 hours
Terrain: Moderately hilly
Surface: Good
Things to see: Aqua Circus, Judah Baker Windmill, Yarmouth Herring Run

Start this ride by parking your car in the parking lot of the Home Federal Savings Bank on the southeast corner of Route 28 (Main Street) and Berry Avenue. Proceed across 28 and go north on Higgins Crowell Road. A sign will point to ROUTE 6. Go through the typical Cape Cod pine forest here, uphill for 0.8 mile to the juncture with Buck Island Road; turn right. This is a well-paved two-lane road that goes by cranberry bogs, off to the right. Come to West Yarmouth Road. Turn left on this two-lane road. Pass through patches of open countryside, still climbing, as you go inland from the shore. Three miles into the ride you come to Old Town House Road; turn right. There is a country feeling out here where the land is sparsely settled. Old Town House Road is a big three-lane road still going uphill. In 1.25 miles turn right on Station Avenue, a gently rolling road, which goes mostly downhill.

Just past the regional high school on your left, across the football field, turn right onto Long Pond Drive. Skirt Long Pond, which you can glimpse through the trees to your left. At the end of Long Pond, after passing Winslow Gray Road on the right, turn left on Mercury Drive. At the point where Venus Road comes in from the right and Mars Lane also goes off at an angle to the right, continue straight ahead on Mercury Drive, which will T into Lyman Lane. Turn right on little Lyman Lane and go down to Route 28, turn left and then immediately right onto Wood Lane. Go past a small, wooded lane divider where there's a statue of a fireman. Just past this spot, turn right onto Wood Road, a narrow residential street. Cross Main Street (Route 28); the road you're on is now called River Street, which takes you down to and briefly along the Bass River.

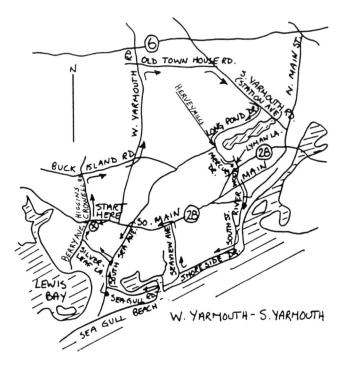

W. YARMOUTH - S. YARMOUTH

How to get there: From the west take U.S. 6 to Route 132, 132 south to 28, and 28 east to West Yarmouth, to Berry Avenue. The Yarmouth Police Station is on the northwest corner.

At the fork with Pleasant Street, bear right on River Street. Soon after the fork, you will come to the Judah Baker Windmill on the bank of Bass River in tiny Windmill Park. There's a nice little beach here. The windmill was originally built in 1791 in South Dennis and moved here in 1863. The town now owns it and is restoring it. Continue on River Street, which swings around ninety degrees to the right and then comes to South Street, where there's a stop sign. Turn left onto South Street, which takes you down to Shore Side Drive. Run Pond is on your right. Smuggler's or Bass River Beach is here on the curve just as you get to the shore line. There are lots of motels, cottages, and quiet houses. You are now on Shore Side Drive. Proceed along the waterfront. There are houses between you and the water, but you can go down any one of the streets running off to your left to the shore. Several public beaches can be found along this road.

At the stop sign at Seaview Avenue, turn left past the Beach House Motor Lodge to the point, a nice place to take a break and get a great, unimpeded view of the ocean. Turn around and go straight up Seaview Avenue to Main Street, on Route 28. At the stop sign turn left. The Aqua Circus is on the right. They have six shows a day, featuring dolphins. Just past the Aqua Circus comes South Sea Avenue and a traffic light, where you turn left and return to the shore line.

Sea Gull Road comes up in a mile; turn left onto it and head for Sea Gull Beach. Lewis Pond will be in sight to your left. Stretches of the road become a causeway across the marshes. Beautiful Sea Gull Beach is open from 8:00 a.m. to 10:00 p.m. There are rest room facilities. After your swim and/or picnic, return to South Sea Avenue via Sea Gull Road. Turn right on South Sea and then, about four blocks up, turn left onto Silver Leaf Lane, which will take you 0.6 mile to Berry Avenue. There is a stop sign, but there may not be a street sign; however, you'll be able to identify it because Silver Leaf Lane jogs to the left after it crosses Berry. Turn right on Berry, which will take you back up to South Main Street, where you started your ride.

9. West Dennis — Harwichport

Number of miles: 18
Approximate pedaling time: 2 hours
Terrain: Flat to moderately hilly
Surface: Good
Things to see: Towns of Harwich and Harwichport, Cape Cod Rail Trail, Allen Harbor, Glendon Beach, Swan River, West Dennis Beach

Start this ride in the parking lot of the Ezra H. Baker Public School on the corner of Route 28 and Trotting Park Road.

Leave the parking lot and turn right, heading north on Trotting Park Road. A stop sign comes up shortly at the intersection with Center Street. You should see a sign here that indicates OLD MAIN STREET to the left. You continue across and to the right forty-five degrees onto a paved, wide, two-lane road. You'll pass Pine Field Lane and Lockwood Drive and a well-preserved old Congregational church. Bear left at the small island with an equally small stone marker, past a public library to the intersection with High Bank Road, also called Great Western Road. A building called Liberty Hall is on the opposite corner; turn right and go the short distance to the traffic light at Route 134. With great caution go straight across Route 134 and turn left onto a bike path on the right side of the road. Ride about 0.25 mile to the well-marked entrance to the Cape Cod Rail Trail. You now will have a 4.5-mile, traffic-free ride all the way to Route 124. When you reach 124, turn off the trail and ride down 124 approximately 1 mile to Main Street in Harwich; turn left on Main.

Riding along on Main Street, watch for Bank Street as you enjoy Harwichport, which is a picturesque village with old houses and a pleasant air.

Leaving Harwichport on Bank Street, there is a good downhill run to Harwich past cranberry bogs here and there, for a nice 1.5-mile ride. At the junction of Route 28 and Bank Street turn right and ride west on 28 until the fork where Route 28 goes off to the right and Lower County Road bears left. (If you have time, take a detour down to Wychmere Harbor by turning left when

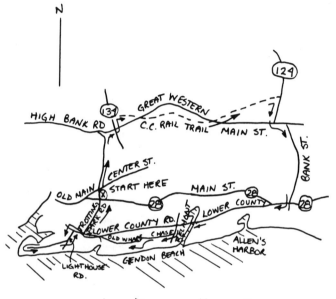

WEST DENNIS - HARWICHPORT

How to get there: From the west take Route 6 to Route 134 in South Dennis. Take 134 south to Route 28, turn right onto Route 28 and proceed three-eights of a mile to the intersection of Route 28 and Trotting Park Road.

Bank Street comes to a T at Route 28 and going east for about a quarter of a mile to Wychmere Road. Turn right. Enjoy your visit to this scenic harbor, and then return to Route 28, head west, and continue the bike trail.) You take Lower County Road.

Ride through Harwichport with its interesting old houses, churches, and little shops. Continue past Allen's Harbor, a tiny protected harbor right off the road, and over the Herring River into Dennisport, where you'll see some of the southernmost part of that town. There is a lovely view of the harbor, the docks, and the windmill out on the point. This is a nice place to stop.

Turn left on Belmont Road and at the end of it turn right on Chase Avenue where the road parallels Motel Mecca. Follow closely when it goes right and then turn immediately left onto Old Wharf Road. At the five-way intersection, cross Sea Street and continue straight ahead on Old Wharf Road, and you'll come upon Glendon Beach, which is public. Old Wharf Road ends at the stop sign at Lower County Road; turn left.

Shortly afterward cross over the Swan River with its fascinating marsh lands. Turn left onto Lighthouse Road. There will be a sign to the Town Beach right across from a marsh; continue down to the extensive and beautiful West Dennis Public Beach. When you're ready to go, return up Lighthouse Road to Lower County Road and turn right. Ride as far as Trotting Park Road; turn left. Ride 1 mile back to your starting place at Route 28 and Trotting Park Road.

10. Harwich — West Chatham

Number of miles: 14
Approximate pedaling time: 2 hours
Terrain: Rolling hills
Surface: Good
Things to see: Town of Harwich, Brooks Free Library, Town Beach, Cockle Cove, Ridgevale Beach, central Cape Cod countryside

Start your ride in the center of Harwich, on Main Street, near the juncture of routes 39 and 124.

Harwich is a lovely, small, New England town with its graceful white Congregational church. It has some five antique shops on its Main Street—great for browsing. If you have pannier bags you might find that small gee-gaw you've looked for everywhere.

Ride east on Main Street, past the Brooks Free Library. You might stop in here to see the collection of nineteenth-century statuary by John Roger. They are set in a Victorian atmosphere. Then you pass the bandstand and ball field to a Y where you will bear right on Chatham Road. Main Street is lined with trees that are larger and taller than those found closer to the sea. One and a half miles down Chatham Road, you'll come to a T intersection with Route 28. Turn right on 28 and ride a short distance to Deep Hole Road; turn left and ride 0.5 mile down to the small but lovely town beach. There are rest rooms here. When you're ready to leave, take the road that starts just across from the rest rooms. This is Uncle Venies Road, although it may not be so marked.

Ride up 0.25 mile and turn right onto South Chatham Road. The route is parallel to the beach and ocean here and provides a fine view across the salt marsh. Pass Soundview coming in from the left. Once you pass over into Chatham, this road becomes Deep Hole Road, although there might not be a sign. The road goes uphill for a short distance, and then levels off just before the T intersection with Pleasant Street. There's a stop sign here. Turn left onto Pleasant Street and ride up to Route 28. Turn right onto 28, where you'll see a village store and snack bar on the corner.

How to get there: From the west take Route 6 to Route 124 in the township of Harwich. Go right on 124 to the center of Harwich.

This is a rolling road. Follow it for 0.75 mile, past Route 137, which comes in from the left, to Cockle Cove Road. There's a sign saying COCKLE COVE; turn right and go down to the cove and Ridgevale Beach.

After visiting the beach, retrace the route back up the same road to Route 28, where you turn right and then left on Sam Ryders Road. It's mostly uphill here for almost 1 mile to a T intersection with Queen Anne Road. Turn left here. Stay on Queen Anne Road for 4 miles, to the intersection with Route 124. Queen Anne Road is not well marked, so follow the map and instructions carefully. Pass Church Street and then cross Route 137, which bends here and is called Morton Road on your left and Long Pond on your right. Continue straight, and soon Cemetery Road will come in from your right and merge into Queen Anne Road. Stay on Queen Anne. You'll come to a stop sign on Route 39; cross over and continue past a small pond, and then Bucks Pond and Josephs Pond, all on your left. Just past the ponds, the road widens. At the intersection of Queen Anne Road and Route 124, there is a stop sign. Turn left onto Route 124, which is called Pleasant Lake Road. From here the route is mostly downhill for 1 mile to Harwich and your starting place.

11. The Cape Cod Rail Trail

Number of miles: 19.6
Approximate pedaling time: $2^1/_2$ hours
Terrain: Flat to moderately hilly
Surface: Excellent
Things to see: Fresh water lakes (called ponds), forests,
fresh water marshes, cranberry bogs, Rock Harbor and all the
flora and fauna contained therein

This unique ride is off the road, on its own 8-foot-wide bicycle
"street," for 17.5 of its total length of 19.6 miles. Except for a short
distance on West Road in Orleans to pass over Route 6 and for
2.1 miles on Main Street and Rock Harbor Road, also in Orleans,
it runs along the abandoned right-of-way of the old Penn Central
Railroad from Route 134 in South Dennis to Locust Road in
Eastham, ending 0.25 mile from the Salt Pond Visitors' Center. The
original railroad was built in the early 1880s and finally abandoned for railroading purposes in 1965.

Since there are parking lots at each end of the trail as well
as at Route 124 in Harwich and Nickerson State Park in Brewster,
you could begin your ride at any one of these points. Rest areas
and comfort stations can be found at the Dennis Town Hall just
west of the Route 134 terminus, on Old Bass River Road,
Nickerson State Park, the Salt Pond Visitors' Center, and at most
town beaches.

If you decide to start at the Route 134 end, as you travel
along the trail you will pass many fresh water ponds, created
thousands of years ago by tremendous blocks of ice left behind
by the retreating glacier. Sand Pond, Hinkley's Pond, Seymour,
and Long Pond are a few of these "kettle" ponds you will pass. At
the intersection with Route 6A in Brewster you will come alongside Nickerson State Park, 1,750 acres, with four ponds ranging in
size from 18 to 204 acres, over 400 campsites, and 8 miles of bike
paths. Just past the park the trail will go under Route 6A through
its own small tunnel and enter the area of salt marshes such as
the NAMSKAKET CREEK, a classic example of a barrier beach salt

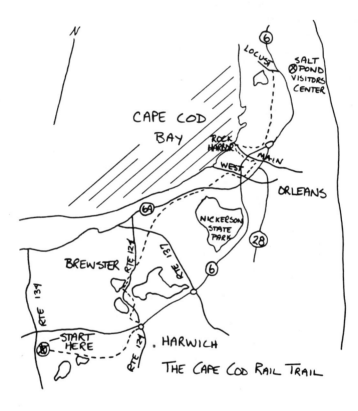

N

CAPE COD
BAY

LOCUST

6

SALT
⊗ POND
VISITORS
CENTER

ROCK
HARBOR

MAIN

WEST

ORLEANS

6A

NICKERSON
STATE
PARK

28

BREWSTER

RTE 124

RTE 137

6

RTE 134

START
HERE

137

RTE 134

HARWICH

THE CAPE COD RAIL TRAIL

How to get there: For the west end (Route 134), take Route 6 to Route 134 and go south to the entrance to the trail. For the east end (Eastham), take Route 6 to the Salt Pond Visitors' Center in Eastham.

marsh system, which will be on your left. After this when the trail reaches Orleans, it will take you out onto Main Street, where you turn left and ride through the Orleans business district with shops of all kinds (plus motorized vehicles—so be alert!). It's a short detour down to Rockport Harbor, a small fishing harbor with a beach for swimming. When you leave this neat place, turn left (a left-hand turn facing inland), paralleling Route 6. The bike trail soon reappears on the left side of the road. Farther north the fresh water ponds reappear and the ride ends at Locust Road in Eastham, 0.25 mile from the Salt Pond Visitors' Center on Route 6. This beautiful facility of the Cape Cod National Seashore blends artistically into the landscape and through its exhibits and films provides a fascinating glimpse into the human and natural history of the Cape—plus giving you a breathtaking view of a tremendous salt pond.

12. West Brewster — Dennis

Number of miles: 21
Approximate pedaling time: 3 hours
Terrain: Hilly
Surface: Good to excellent
Things to see: Stony Brook Grist Mill, Chapin Memorial Beach, New England Fire and History Museum, Sesuit Neck Harbor, Sealand, The Drummer Boy Museum, Museum of Natural History and Smock Windmill, Josiah Dennis Manse

Begin this ride on Route 6A just west of Route 137 (Long Pond Road). Park in the lot of the New England Fire and History Museum. Come out of the parking lot and turn right onto Main Street (Route 6A). At the fork where 6A goes right, take the left hand, which is Stony Brook Road. There's also a sign indicating a bike route in this direction. You'll pass Smith Pond on the left and then a series of ponds.

You'll soon begin a stiff uphill and then take a steep downhill. About 0.75 mile from the fork you'll come upon the Stony Brook Mill on the left. This grist mill still works to show you how it was done. It is open from 2:00 to 5:00 p.m. Wednesdays, Fridays, and Saturdays in July and August.

There is a fork just beyond the mill; here, bear left onto Satucket Road—after a couple of miles the road changes its name to Setucket. *Sa* or *Se,* it's still a hilly road. You pass a lovely, placid little pond and go through a forested area. Two miles from the fork of Satucket and Stony Brook roads, there is another pond, where you bear right, remaining on Satucket Road. There is much open, unsettled country here, very much like parts of Connecticut. In another mile cross Route 134. A half mile after 134 you'll come to Old Bass River Road, which has a paved bike path alongside it. Turn right onto the bike path on the right side, and ride the 1.8 miles to Route 6A. The bike path ends about a half mile from 6A. It is downhill here, and Hokum Rock Road and Scargo Road come sweeping in from your right, so exercise lots of caution! Once at 6A, turn left, using the sidewalk, and go about 0.25 mile to where Route 6A turns hard left and where you go right onto

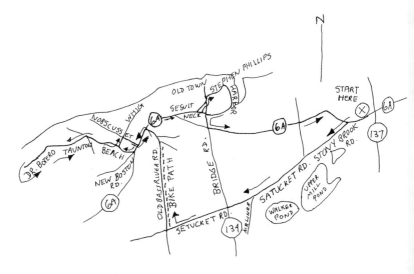

N

WEST BREWSTER - DENNIS

How to get there: From the west take Route 6A just into Brewster and watch for the New England Fire and History Museum on the left, just before the Town Hall. From the east take 6A through Brewster past the intersection of routes 124 and 137 to the museum.

New Boston Road—just after Nobscusset Road and across from the Dennis Public Market. Almost immediately there is a fork with Beach Street; bear right onto Beach. Easy Bay View Street comes in from the right; you go left, heading for Chapin Beach, taking the farthest left road at the three-way fork, which is Taunton Avenue. Taunton soon turns right and then left, and here you will see a sign telling you that this little piece of road is Dr. Botero Road. This is a dune-and-grass area with water on both sides. Continue out through the dunes. Just follow the paved road for as far as it goes and you'll come to Chapin Beach. It's on the bay side of the Cape, so the dunes and waves are smaller but still beautiful.

Return the way you came to Beach Street. Stay on Beach as far as Whig Street on the left. It's the next street after Tory Lane, *bien entendu!* Turn left onto Whig and go to the next intersection, with Nobscusset Road, and turn right. At the corner is the Josiah Dennis Manse, a grey-shingled house built in 1736 for Dennis. Did you know that *manse* means the residence of a minister?

Follow Nobscusset Road back to Route 6A, and then turn left and head east toward East Dennis and Brewster. Ride along 6A, using the sidewalks where available, for slightly more than a mile to the fork with Sesuit Neck Road. You go left onto Sesuit Neck Road while Route 6A goes right without you. Go down Sesuit Neck for about 0.5 mile until Old Town Lane comes in from the left at a little fork with a small traffic island in the center. Go left on Old Town, and then, in a short distance, left again on Bridge Street and soon after, right onto Stephen Phillips Road. Follow Stephen Phillips as it turns left, down to the seashore and right on Harbor Road to Sesuit Neck Harbor. If the weather is fine, the land and seascapes should make this tortuous route worthwhile. Continue around the busy little harbor on Harbor Road until it joins with and becomes Sesuit Neck Road. Continue until the intersection with Bridge Road, where you turn left and go up to Route 6A. Turn left on 6A and ride past the salt marshes into Brewster.

At the intersection where Stony Brook Road goes off to the right, go left. You will be on Main Street, Brewster, as well as Route 6A, and you'll soon come to the starting place at the New England Fire and History Museum.

13. Brewster — Nickerson State Park

Number of miles: 16
Approximate pedaling time: $2^{1}/_{2}$ hours
Terrain: Moderately hilly
Surface: Good
Things to see: Nickerson State Forest, Brewster, Brewster and Harwich countryside

Start this ride in Nickerson State Park just off Route 6A in Brewster. In the summertime the parking lot just inside the entrance to the park is a holding area for campers. After Labor Day you can park here, but in the summer, park either in the parking lot located 1,000 feet west of the entrance, off Route 6A, or go into the park a short distance straight ahead just past the amphitheatre, where there is a parking area on your right.

You can begin the ride here and start off on the bike path to the right. This paved path is just for you, and it winds its way mostly downhill for approximately 2 miles through the park.

Just after you pass the dumping station and the fire tower (off to your left), stay on the bike path as it turns right ninety degrees at an intersection of the park road (which turns left) and three other roads, all of which are outside the park. Access to these by car is barred by a gate. There are several private homes here on Windswept Road and Joe Longs Road. Here the bike path parallels Joe Longs Road. In 0.25 mile leave the park bike path and cross over to Joe Longs Road just before it comes to a T at Millstone Road, and then turn left onto Millstone Road. Ride on Millstone for about 1.5 miles until it tees into Route 137, which is also called Long Pond Road. Turn left and ride 2.5 miles through a forest where the colors are gorgeous in the fall, to the point, just before Route 6, where Long Pond Road goes right ninety degrees. Turn right and ride through scrub pine forests on either side. There will be an occasional glimpse of Long Pond on the right. When Long Pond tees into Route 124, turn right and get on the Cape Cod Rail Trail, which runs along Route 124 here. Take this marvelous bike path north for approximately 5.5 miles as it criss-

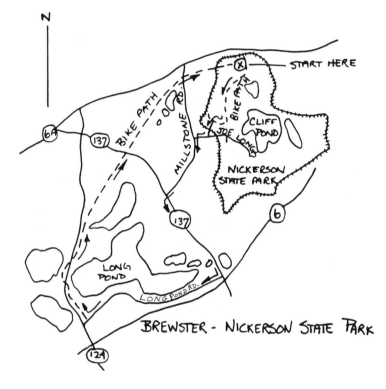

N

START HERE

BIKE PATH

6A

137

MILLSTONE RD.

BIKE PATH

CLIFF POND

JOE LONG

NICKERSON STATE PARK

6

137

LONG POND

LONG POND RD.

BREWSTER - NICKERSON STATE PARK

124

How to get there: Take Route 6A east to Brewster and the entrance to Nickerson State Forest. Coming down 6A from the east, you'll find the state forest on your left about 1.5 miles west of the junction of Routes 6 and 6A.

crosses Route 124 by Long Pond and Seymour Pond and proceeds off to the north through the woods, past the Brewster Golf Club, right up to where it borders the waiting areas in Nickerson State Park. Here you turn right at the small sign NICKERSON STATE PARK and ride the very short distance on this spur of the Cape Cod Rail Trail into the park and return to your starting place. Just after this point, the Rail Trail goes left and under Route 6A, so if you find yourself doing that, you have gone too far.

14. Chatham

Number of miles: 21
Approximate pedaling time: 3 hours
Terrain: Hilly to flat
Surface: Good
Things to see: The beautiful town and harbors of Chatham, Chatham Fish Pier, Chatham Lighthouse

Begin the ride in the parking lot of the shopping center at the junction of Queen Anne Road and Route 28 in Chatham. It's a five-point intersection. When you leave the parking lot bearing right on Queen Anne Road, you'll be on a marked bike route. At the Y continue right on Pond Street (Queen Anne Road goes up to the left). Circle enormous Oyster Pond, which has a public beach. At the stop sign of the T intersection, turn right onto Stage Harbor Road. At the Y intersection with Cedar Street turn right onto Cedar Street. When Cedar Street comes to a T at Battlefield Road, turn left and ride along Battlefield until the T with Champlain Road. Turn left onto Champlain, still following the bike route. Very soon Champlain makes a ninety-degree bend to the left at the shore of Stage Harbor. You can see Stage Harbor Lighthouse out there as your route takes you along the shore of this beautiful harbor. Look for the nun and can buoys marking the channel. There are fishing boats at Old Mill Boatyard.

Champlain Road turns left and becomes Stage Harbor Road. Bear left, and shortly you will come to a stop sign where Bridge Street is on the right; turn right onto it. There's a nice little dock here. Go over the drawbridge and go straight until you come to a T with Morris Island Road. Turn right to go down Morris Island Road. On the left is the Chatham Lighthouse. When you come to Little Beach Road straight ahead, you bear right, continuing on Morris Island Road. Bear left and down and across the causeway. You're on Morris Island, and when you come to the end of the road you'll see a sign saying QUITNESSET. When you're ready, double back across the dike. At the stop sign continue straight past the Chatham Lighthouse on what is actually Main Street.

Take in the view, looking past Nauset Beach to the Atlantic. Main Street will curve up to the left. There may not be a street

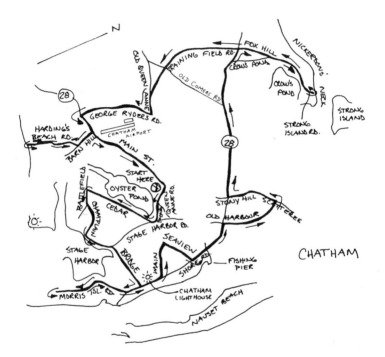

N

OLD QUEEN ANNE RD.

TRAINING FIELD RD.

FOX HILL

NICKERSON'S

CROWS POND

OLD COMERS RD.

CROW'S POND

NECK

STRONG ISLAND

28

GEORGE RYDERS RD.

STRONG ISLAND RD.

HARDINGS BEACH RD.

CHATHAM AIRPORT

BARN HILL

MAIN ST.

28

START HERE

OYSTER POND

QUEEN ANNE RD.

BATTLEFIELD

CHAMPLIN

CEDAR

STAGE HARBOR RD.

STONY HILL

SCATTEREE

OLD HARBOUR

STAGE HARBOR

BRIDGE

MAIN

SEAVIEW

SHORE RD.

FISHING PIER

CHATHAM

MORRIS ISL. RD.

CHATHAM LIGHTHOUSE

NAUSET BEACH

How to get there: From the west take Route 28 directly into Chatham and proceed to the starting place in the center of Chatham.

sign. There is a stop sign across from you and one for traffic coming down from your left but none on your side. Turn left, uphill past all the little shops to the corner of Seaview and Main. Turn sharply right onto Seaview and go up an incline so steep you can get off and walk with impunity. Continue up and to the right to Shore Road, where you turn left, ride one long block, and turn sharply right at the sign: TOWN OF CHATHAM FISH PIER.

Go back to Shore Road and turn right. At the traffic light Old Harbor Road crosses Shore. Turn right onto Old Harbor Road and go downhill. At the T of Old Harbor and Scatteree roads, turn left on Scatteree, again following the bike route. Bend around to the left, downhill past Old Mail Road, on what is now called Stony Hill Road for about 0.6 mile until you come to Route 28, which is also Orleans Road. There may not be a sign, but it does look like a Route 28, what with a stop sign to hold you back and a Texaco station across the street on your left, so turn right and go downhill. Bear right at the first Y intersection with Old Comers Road and continue to the Y with Crow's Pond Road; turn right and follow Crow's Pond to Fox Hill Road. Bear right onto Fox Hill and take it out to Nickerson's Neck, all the way to Strong Island Road. Turn left and go to the end of the road where it overlooks Strong Island. Backtrack to Fox Hill Road and bear right with a view of Crow's Pond to the left as you ride. At the intersection of Crow's Pond and Fox Hill roads, bear right on Fox Hill. At the stop-sign intersection with Route 28, continue straight across on what is now called Training Field Road. You will cross Old Comers Road. Where Old Queen Anne Road comes in from the right to merge with Training Field Road, you continue, bearing to the left on what is now Old Queen Anne Road.

When George Ryders Road comes in from the right, turn right onto it and follow it to Chatham Airport, which has a restaurant and rest rooms. Continue on George Ryders Road a short distance to Route 28, where you turn left and in about 0.25 mile, come to Barn Hill Road. It should be the second road after your turn onto Route 28. Turn right. This road goes downhill and curves left and right to a Y with Hardings Beach Road. Turn right on Hardings Beach Road and follow it to the beach. This is a public beach with sand dunes. Retrace the route back to Route 28, where you turn right and head back to your starting place.

15. Orleans

Number of miles: 13
Approximate pedaling time: 2 hours
Terrain: Moderately hilly
Surface: Good
Things to see: French Cable Museum, Town Cove, Nauset Harbor, Nauset Beach, Rock Harbor

Start your ride in the Stop & Shop parking lot, which is across from the large Orleans Inn on Routes 6A and 28, just before the Orleans-Eastham town line.

Leave your bike carrier here and ride out to 6A and 28; turn right. You quickly come to a Y intersection where 28 and 6A split. Bear left on Route 28. In 0.3 mile come to Cove Road; turn left and go down the short hill to the shores of Town Cove. The tiny Orleans Yacht Club is located here at the innermost end of this long cove, which is bordered by Orleans and Eastham. Come back up the short but steep hill. You will be turning left here, but first take a look into the French Cable Museum on the corner. The building housed the United States terminus of the original Atlantic cable and is now a museum, open only Friday through Monday, 2:00–4:00 p.m.

Now turn left onto 28 and ride to Main Street where you turn ninety degrees left, on your way to Nauset Beach. Another short ride brings you to the intersection of Main Street and Tonset Road. Turn left onto Tonset. Over on your left there is a nice view of Town Cove. Continue on Tonset past woods on the left and characteristic Cape Cod houses on the right, past Gibson Road and Brick Hill Road, straight out to the dead end where Tonset Road overlooks Nauset Harbor, which is a cut through Nauset Beach. This is 3.5 miles from your starting point.

Turn around and go back up Tonset Road to Brick Hill Road and turn left. Continue on Brick Hill as it twists and turns, passing by Champlain and Hopkins Lane and through wooded areas that are alive with color in the fall. About 1.5 miles from your turn onto Brick Hill, there is a T intersection with Beach Road. Unfortunately you may not see a street sign here, but it is

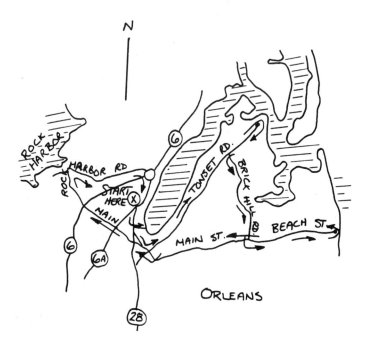

How to get there: From the south take 28 or 6A a short distance past the point where they merge in Orleans to the Orleans Inn. Turn left into the large parking lot across from the inn.

Beach Road; so turn left and in 0.6 mile, over to your right, you will feast your eyes on a stunning vista of the salt marshes with the beach in the distance.

From here to the beach it is downhill; once there you will find a large parking lot, dressing rooms, rest rooms, telephone, a small refreshment stand plus one gorgeous beach where you can swim, picnic, and/or walk in the dunes. Come back up the hill, retracing your route. Pass the intersection with Brick Hill Road and continue straight on Beach Road, passing the Raleigh Neck Inn and then, at a Y intersection with Main Street, bear to the right onto Main.

You'll pass the Orleans Theater and come to a stoplight at the intersection of Main and Tonset. Continue on Main Street, crossing Route 28 and then 6A. You are passing through the Orleans business district with shops of all kinds as you head toward the bay side and Rock Harbor. This is a tiny, bustling harbor, chock-full of fishing boats for professional fishermen and for amateurs. It's a very businesslike place with a restaurant and convenient dockside parking lot. The Cape Cod Rail Trail detours through Rockport, so expect to see lots of fellow riders.

Next, take Rock Harbor Road around to the left—a left-hand turn facing inland—and you'll soon find yourself paralleling Route 6. You will also pass a section of the off-road Cape Cod Rail Trail that begins again off to your left. Just past the Eastham-Orleans town line turn right at the rotary, continuing around it till you reach the entrance to a small shopping center with a Wendy's; turn in here to take a shortcut around the back of Stop & Shop to your starting place.

16. Eastham — Coast Guard Beach

Number of miles: 9.7
Approximate pedaling time: $1^1/_2$ hours
Terrain: Moderately hilly
Surface: Good
Things to see: Salt Pond Visitors' Center, Eastham Historical Society Museum, Eastham Windmill, Great Pond, Nauset Light Beach, Coast Guard Beach

Start the ride in the parking lot of the Salt Pond Visitors' Center, where you can leave your motorized vehicle, if you have one. There are two of these visitors' centers in the National Park Service's Cape Cod National Seashore, and both are beautifully designed and integrated architecturally into the landscape. Not only do they provide you with fascinating information about the human and natural history of the surrounding area through exhibits and illustrated orientation programs, but situated as they are on high ground, they afford marvelous vistas of the seashore.

The Salt Pond Visitors' Center overlooks the quite amazing and beautiful landscape of an enormous salt pond. Plan to spend at least several hours at the center upon your return. Be sure to explore a bit of the Braille Nature Trail before you leave the parking lot. Proceed toward Route 6, past the Eastham Historical Society Museum on the right. It's open Wednesday and Friday afternoons in July and August.

Cross over Route 6 at the light and continue straight ahead on Locust Road to the beginning of the Cape Cod Rail Trail on the left. Ride along the straight bike path for about half a mile until you come to the first crossing, Samoset Road. Turn left and go up the short distance to the Eastham Windmill, which is in the small, triangular-shaped park. It still works! Turn around and come back down Samoset Road, past the Cape Cod Rail Trail to Great Pond Road, where you turn right. If you'd like to take a short side trip to the Cape Cod. Bayside, continue straight ahead to First Encounter Beach. Return to Great Pond Road and proceed past the Town Landing and public beach on the shore of Great Pond. If you'd like a swim in the warmer waters of a lake, try this one.

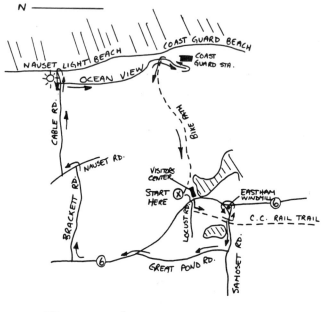

N

COAST GUARD BEACH

NAUSET LIGHT BEACH

OCEAN VIEW

COAST GUARD STA.

CABLE RD.

BIKE PATH

BRACKETT RD.

NAUSET RD.

VISITORS CENTER

START HERE

LOCUST RD.

EASTHAM WINDMILL

C.C. RAIL TRAIL

SANOSET RD.

6

GREAT POND RD.

EASTHAM - COAST GUARD BEACH

How to get there: Take Route 6 from the north or south into Eastham. Watch for the sign SALT POND VISITORS' CENTER.

Go uphill from Great Pond, continuing on Great Pond Road through a residential part of Eastham, back to Route 6, which will be about 1 mile from your turn onto this road from Samoset Road. When you arrive at Route 6, turn left and ride along the "bi-walk," an extra-wide sidewalk shared by pedestrians and bicyclists. In 0.75 mile, at the traffic light at Brackett Road, you'll see a large green sign, NAUSET LIGHT BEACH—your next destination. Proceed across 6 and uphill on Brackett Road. In 1 mile at the T intersection with Nauset Road, turn left and then immediately right onto Cable Road to a bluff overlooking the ocean and Nauset Light Beach. In the event that the Nauset and Cable Road signs are missing, watch for the signs to Nauset Light Beach. The beach is below the bluff. As you leave the beach parking lot, turn left at the first intersection, Ocean View Drive. When Coast Guard Beach comes into sight, there is a sudden downhill at the bottom of which you must yield, so watch the traffic, then cross over the wooden bridge to the parking lot behind the former Coast Guard station. From the observation areas to the side and front of the large white building, the view of the ocean and the tidal wetlands is spectacular. If you can get back here at sunset, do; the display of glorious colors is stunning.

After you have seen and experienced all you have time for, take the bike path that begins just behind the former four-boat garage which now houses changing and rest rooms.The bike path (or trail, as the National Seashore people call it) crosses two spur roads, and just before the first one you'll see the Doane Rock and picnic site. This lovely bike trail will take you 2 miles, mostly downhill, back to the Salt Pond Visitors' Center.

17. South Wellfleet—Marconi Station

Number of miles: 9.6
Approximate pedaling time: $1^1/_2$ hours
Terrain: Moderately hilly
Surface: Very good
Things to see: The Marconi Wireless Station, Marconi Beach, the Audubon Society's Wildlife Sanctuary, The Cape Cod National Seashore Headquarters

Leave your automobile in the parking lot of the Cape Cod National Seashore Headquarters and ride out toward the ocean and the Marconi Station site. This is very flat, almost like a plain. Then the road goes gently uphill to the top of a bluff. Here, on this bluff, Guglielmo Marconi built his wireless station and sent the first wireless telegraph message across the Atlantic to England in 1903, a message from President Teddy Roosevelt to King Edward VII. There is a display that tells the fascinating story. Lock up your bike and take a nature trail to White Cedar Swamp and Forest, crossing the swamp on a boardwalk.

Retrace your road back, past the C.C.N.S. Headquarters to the park; turn left and head toward Marconi Beach. This great beach is another of the lovingly preserved, fine white sand beaches of *your* Cape Cod National Seashore, stretching as far as the eye can see. The bathhouse facilities are designed low and of weathered grey board to complement, not intrude upon, the landscape. There is a boardwalk with steps leading down to the beach.

When you are ready to continue, return, pass the headquarters again, and proceed to Route 6. Turn left onto Route 6 and proceed for 1.5 miles until you see the white and green sign featuring a herring gull, stating MASS. AUDUBON SOCIETY. Turn right and go straight ahead into the society's Wellfleet Bay Wildlife Sanctuary. It's open from 8:00 a.m. to 8:00 p.m., and there is a small fee. When you reach the parking area, you'll notice a pipe sticking up out of the ground which has a slot in it—and it is into this pipe that you deposit your fee!

There are picnic tables, rest rooms, and a bike road. Try to plan your day so that you have ample time to explore the nature

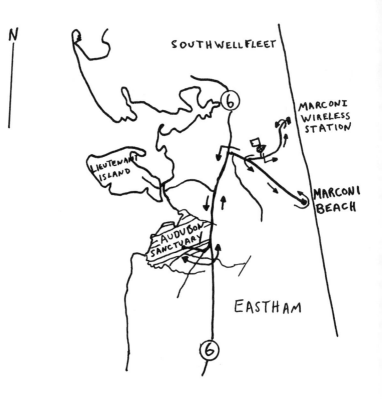

N

SOUTH WELLFLEET

MARCONI
WIRELESS
STATION

LIEUTENANT
ISLAND

MARCONI
BEACH

AUDUBON
SANCTUARY

EASTHAM

How to get there: Proceed north on Route 6 to South Wellfleet. About 1.75 miles from the Eastham town line turn right after the sign MARCONI AREA NEXT RIGHT. Proceed a half mile to the Cape Cod National Seashore Headquarters.

trail on foot. If you go to the office, in the house to your left, you can pick up a map of the sanctuary. The area that is particularly exciting for nature lovers is Try Island, out in the marsh. Here you can see a landscape that is particularly characteristic of the Cape and of the New England shore—great tidal wetlands. The island permits you to go out far into the marsh and experience the space, color, smell, and rhythm of the wetlands. If you buy guides for the sanctuary's specific walks, you will be greatly assisted in identifying the rich birdlife and flora of the marsh and woodlands. This is one of the few sites on the Cape that provides access to the wetlands.

When you leave the sanctuary, turn left at the gate and within a few yards you'll rejoin Route 6. Proceed for 1 mile back to the C.C.N.S. Headquarters. Before you leave, go inside the building. It has exhibits, a supply of informative pamphlets, some very friendly and helpful U.S. National Park Service people—and rest rooms.

18. South Wellfleet — Lecount Hollow

Number of miles: 9.7
Approximate pedaling time: 1 hour
Terrain: Definitely hilly
Surface: Good
Things to see: Typical Cape pine forest, Lecount Hollow Beach, Ocean View Beach, White Crest Beach, bluffs

Park in the restaurant's parking lot and head south down Route 6 about 0.5 mile. Just past the cemetery on your left, turn left on Cahoon Hollow Road. Go uphill. It's short but very steep. Take the second road on the right, which is Old County Road. You will meander through a semi-residential area of dunes and a typical Cape pine forest. Old County Road is roughly parallel to Route 6. After about 1.5 miles Bell Road comes in from the right. Continue straight ahead and rejoin Route 6. Turn left on Route 6 and ride about 0.25 mile and turn left onto Lecount Hollow Road. Ride straight to the ocean on this road. Lecount Hollow Beach will be at your feet. This is a lovely white beach bordered by the Cape's very special green and blue ocean. You can swim here, or you may prefer to swim a little farther north of here, off Ocean View Drive where there's a bit more privacy.

Head back down Lecount Hollow Road for a brief stretch to Ocean View Drive. Turn right. The crest yields a sensational view of beach, ocean, and the bluffs dotted with summer cottages (some for rent; most private). There is a parking lot here, so ride in, lock your bike, and walk down to White Crest Beach. You can wander on foot all over the bluffs; you'll see numerous trails heading off through the scrub. Continue on Ocean View Drive after your swim.

When Cahoon Hollow Road crosses Ocean View, you could detour briefly by taking a right down the steep hill to the Town Landing. If you prefer not to, continue straight for a nice long downhill giving you stunning views off to your right.

Turn left on Gross Hill Road, which is very hilly, including a long uphill grade after the fork with Gull Pond Road. (Depending on the time of year, the Gross Hill Road sign may be missing, taken as a souvenir, so, if you pass the turnoff onto Gross Hill you

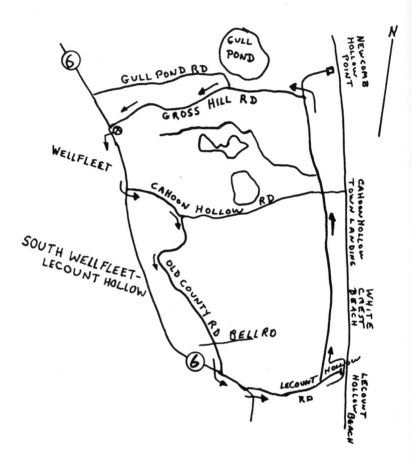

How to get there: Head toward Wellfleet on Route 6.
Watch for Schooner's Cove restaurant on the southeast
corner of the Route 6—Gross Hill Road intersection.
There is a sign saying NEWCOMB HOLLOW—OCEAN BEACH.

will quickly come to a dead end at Newcomb Hollow Point. Go back and take the first road to the right, which is Gross Hill Road.) After about 2 miles on Gross Hill Road you'll return to the intersection where you left your car.

19. Wellfleet — Great Island

Number of miles: 6.8
Approximate pedaling time: 45 minutes
Terrain: Hilly
Surface: Good
Things to see: Wellfleet, Wellfleet Harbor, Mayo Beach, Chequessett Neck, Great Island

Park in the lot next to the Wellfleet Town Hall. Come out onto Main Street and turn left, riding 0.25 mile to a hairpin turn to the right onto East Commerce Street, which takes you down to Wellfleet Harbor, a large, beautifully protected anchorage that you can see in the distance. Ride out to the end of the pier at Shirttail Point to get the full effect of the village, the harbor (watched over by a white, spired church on a hill), and the dunes of Great Island, a preserve of the Cape Cod National Seashore.

Upon leaving the pier, take Kendrick Avenue west along the shore. As in every town on the Cape here you'll pass an abundance of guest houses and motels. Bear left at the junction with Hiller Street and cross the Herring River. At the top of the hill, turn left into the Cape Cod National Seashore picnic grove and parking area. Here you will find guides to the hiking trail on Great Island. This trail is an 8-mile round trip, which you may want to do, provided you have hiking boots and good health. In any event walk some distance onto Great Island just to enjoy the ambience of this unique natural site. Before returning to town you might want to go north downhill on Griffin Island Road to the parking area. Here you can wander along a more remote beach.

To return to town, retrace your route along Chequessett Neck Road. Bear left at the Y, staying on Chequessett Neck Road. Chequessett Neck bears sharply right where Hamblin Farm Road comes in from your left. Stay on Chequessett Neck Road. At the T intersection with Holbrook Road turn left and return to Main Street where you turn right and go the short distance to the Town Hall.

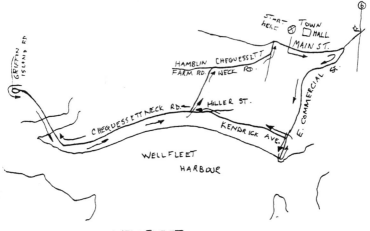

WELLFLEET - GREAT ISLAND

How to get there: From the south take Route 6 past Marconi Beach and Cahoon Hollow Road to the intersection of Long Pond Road (right) and Main Street (left) and a sign WELLFLEET. Turn left onto Main Street, bearing right at the fork with East Commerce Street, and proceed to the Town Hall on the right, where you can park. If you come from the north, the turn onto Main from Route 6 will be a right.

20. North Truro — The Highlands

Number of miles: 9.8
Approximate pedaling time: $1^{1}/_{2}$ hours
Terrain: Cape Cod hills
Surface: Good
Things to see: Head of Meadow Beach, Highland Light, Highland Museum, Jenny Lind Tower, both coasts of the Cape

High Head Road becomes a dirt road soon after it leaves Route 6, at the point where it forks. Here you go left, following the sign that reads PARKING. At the end of this road is a tiny parking lot with a sign at its far end that reads OVER SAND ROUTES—ANNUAL PERMIT REQUIRED. Hidden to the right is the entrance to the Head of the Meadow Bicycle Trail. Start the ride here and take off on your bike onto the fine, paved, bikes-only trail, which wanders through the sand dunes along the edge of Salt Meadow. It runs for a marvelous 2 miles and comes out at Head of Meadow Beach. After a visit to the beach, ride down Head of Meadow Beach Road toward Route 6. When you reach Route 6, turn left and then go off Route 6 to the right, down a short hill, and then left onto Highland Road, which passes under Route 6. You'll see a sign here to HIGHLANDS—1 MILE.

Highlands means just that, so expect a long incline that levels off in a half mile and then continues up a slight grade to a T intersection with a sign that reads HIGHLAND LIGHT. Turn right, go up a short hill, and then turn left. You can see the Highland Lighthouse ahead of you. The Highland House Museum is on your left. Run by the Truro Historical Society, it contains everyday articles used by the Pilgrims (e.g., firearms, relics from shipwrecks). It is open from 1:30 to 4:30 p.m. daily in the summer; a small admission fee is charged. Continue up to the Highland Light (also called the Cape Cod Light). It now flashes a four million–candlepower beacon, warning ships, now mostly huge, heavily laden oil tankers, away from the "Graveyard of Ships."

It was originally built in 1798 then destroyed by fire and rebuilt in 1857. From the overlook you can see both sides of the Cape, ocean and bay. As you walk to the overlook you'll see the

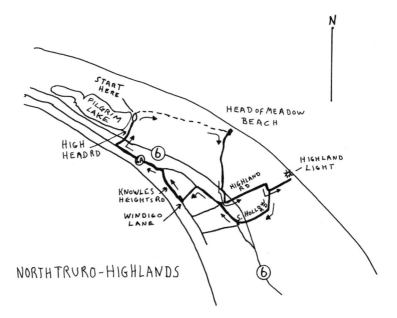

N

START HERE

PILGRIM LAKE

HIGH HEAD RD

HEAD OF MEADOW BEACH

6A

6

HIGHLAND LIGHT

HIGHLAND RD

KNOWLES HEIGHTS RD

WINDIGO LANE

S. HOLLOW

NORTH TRURO-HIGHLANDS

6

How to get there: From the south take Route 6 to High Head Road, at the eastern end of Pilgrim Lake. Depending on the season, the High Head Road sign may be missing, so watch for the sign reading TO RTE. 6A BEACH POINTS, with a left pointing arrow. Turn right just after that sign.

Jenny Lind Tower—a quirky thing!—and beyond the tower, like enormous, frightfully expensive golf balls, the radar domes of an Air Force Radar Station. In 1850 Jenny Lind, the "Swedish Night-ingale," came to Boston for a concert. More tickets were sold than there were seats. To prevent a riot, Jenny climbed to the top of this tower, so the story goes, and sang to the crowd. In 1927 one Harry Aldrich bought the tower and moved it here.

Retrace your tracks and go downhill to the intersection, where you turn left on South Highland Road and run downhill. At the bottom of the grade turn right on South Hollow Road. This is a pleasant road, with no houses on either side, which winds its quiet way through stunted pines for a mile, until it comes to Route 6. Go across Route 6 to the T intersection with Route 6A, just a few feet from 6, and turn right. This is a pretty stiff uphill for 0.25 mile, at which point the road crests and starts to roll up and down.

At approximately 1.2 miles from your turn onto 6A you'll come to Windigo Lane on the left. Turn left onto it. (Disregard the PRIVATE WAY part of the Windigo Lane street sign.) You are on a bluff; wind around for a short stretch, to Cobb Road. Turn left onto Cobb and then right where it tees with Knowles Heights Road. Stay on Knowles Heights Road as it wanders for 1.5 miles through these dunes, along the Cape Cod Bay shore, until it rejoins 6A at the bottom of the short steep downgrade. Where 6A intersects with Route 6, turn left and then right where you see the sign HIGH HEAD. Go up High Head Road to the parking lot where you left your car.

21. Province Lands

Number of miles: 8.75
Approximate pedaling time: 1 hour
Terrain: Hilly
Surface: Excellent
Things to see: Herring Cove Beach, spectacular sand dunes, ponds, bogs, Race Point Beach, Province Lands Visitors' Center

This ride is on a specially laid out asphalt bike path that takes you up and down some spectacular sand dunes and scrub pine forests to the Atlantic Ocean side of the tip of the Cape and then loops back through dramatically contrasting terrain.

When we rode it, in September after Labor Day, we turned left at the first fork, just past the first underpass under Province Lands Road, and went clockwise around the circuit. The Cape Cod National Seashore staff recommends a counter-clockwise circuit from this first fork, however. In summer, when more bikers are in blossom, it is probably wiser to follow their suggestion, although the path is wide enough to pass other bicyclists. There are some great downhills with sharp curves; keep to the right and stay alert.

The area you are passing through was set aside by the Plimouth Colony in 1620, a remarkable act on the part of these hardy folk, preoccupied as they must have been with sheer survival. There are several places to stop and spend some pleasurable time picnicking and/or swimming at either of the two beaches, visiting the Province Lands Visitors' Center, taking the nature walk in the Beach Forest area, or taking a bargain-priced sightseeing flight from the Provincetown Municipal Airport.

The visitors' center is up a steep hill from either direction, and the panoramic view from the observation deck is breathtaking. There is an outdoor theater (closed after Labor Day), and inside movies about the area and its wildlife are shown every hour on the hour.

The Beach Forest Trail is a 1-mile loop that is well worth taking. Be sure you can lock your bike securely before you set out afoot. The walk is beautifully described in detail in *Short Walks on Cape Cod and the Vineyard* by Hugh and Heather Sadlier (Globe Pequot Press).

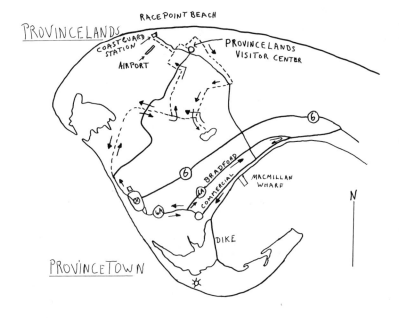

How to get there: Take Route 6 out to the very end of the Cape. Go around the traffic circle to the Herring Cove Beach parking lot.

This is one of the nicest rides on the Cape, with short, roller-coaster hills, unique scenery, and *no* automobiles to contend with.

22. Provincetown

Number of miles: 8.5
Approximate pedaling time: $1^1/_2$ hours
Terrain: Slightly hilly
Surface: Good
Things to see: The myriad wonders of Provincetown! Macmillan Wharf, Provincetown Aquarium, Provincetown Playhouse, Pilgrim Monument and Museum, Seth Nickerson House, Herring Cove Beach

This ride will take you on a tour of fabulous Provincetown with its old houses, historic landmarks, fishing fleet, and artists and artisans of all descriptions. After riding from Herring Cove Beach to the rotary, before you enter the town proper, lock up your bike and walk out on the dike built to protect Provincetown Harbor. The dike, which goes over to Long Point, yields a fine view of the harbor.

The street coming out of Provincetown to this point is one-way, so you can't use it; instead, continue around the rotary, retracing your route to the point where 6A heads into town. Turn right at 6A South—PROVINCETOWN CENTER—BOSTON. This is West Bradford Street. There are two principal streets in Provincetown: Bradford Street, which is two-way, and Commercial Street, which parallels the harbor and is one-way.

As you ride along Bradford, you'll pass numerous little lanes running between Bradford and Commercial. (You will be returning along the waterfront on Commercial Street.) Bradford is lined with guest houses of all shapes, sizes, and qualities and with little restaurants. Pass the David Fairbanks House (1776) and the Folk Museum. At Winslow Street, 3 miles from the start of the ride, turn left and ride up to the Pilgrim Monument and Museum.

As you come to the end of Bradford, you'll pass craft shops, and there will be dozens more of these on Commercial Street. At the junction with Commercial, make a hairpin turn to the right and head back along the waterfront. At this end of town many little cottages are jammed cheek-to-jowl along the road.

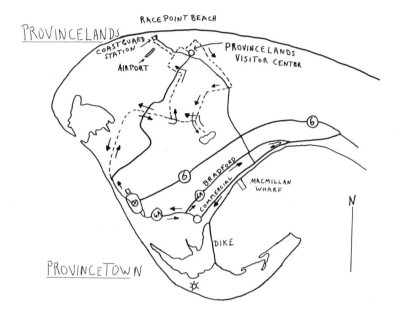

PROVINCELANDS

RACE POINT BEACH

COAST GUARD STATION

AIRPORT

PROVINCELANDS VISITOR CENTER

6

6

BRADFORD

COMMERCIAL

MACMILLAN WHARF

6A

DIKE

PROVINCETOWN

N

How to get there: Take Route 6 out to the very end of the Cape. Go around the traffic circle to the Herring Cove Beach parking lot.

About a mile from the Bradford-Commercial intersection, you'll reach the downtown area. There are some older houses sprinkled through the area on the right, as well as such places as the Provincetown Art Association Gallery. Restaurants, galleries, and shops are piled on each other. Leatherwork, silverwork, antique jewelry, paintings, prints, portraits done in a single sitting—all are available here. Throngs of pedestrians make riding in this narrow street almost impossible; you'll probably find you'd rather get off your bike and push it along through the center of town—or, lock it up while you stroll here, joining the vacationers in a snack or drink at such places as the Inn at the Mews or the Café Blasé (located next to one of several bike rental stands).

Macmillan Wharf is at the 5-mile point on the ride. Go out on the wharf, where, if you can be here at 6:00 a.m., you can watch the commercial fishermen and their catches. If you have the time to spare, take a whale watch cruise on one of the boats that offer this unique experience. Down past the wharf there are numerous additional craftspeople and portrait painters. Soon you'll pass Town Hall Square, the famous Provincetown Playhouse, and Union Square with its many shops.

Turn left where Commercial Street goes almost ninety degrees to the left at the 6-mile point. You'll come to the town landing and Provincetown's oldest house, built circa 1746, at 72 Commercial Street. The house is open to the public. This end of Commercial Street has a number of quaint, older houses and a generally more conservative atmosphere than elsewhere, since it is a quiet residential area. A lovely inn, the Red Inn, is located here—it's open year-round and serves dinner nightly.

You'll come out at the rotary at the dike after 6.5 miles. Turn right and continue back toward the car. The ride ends back at Herring Cove Beach at the parking lot.

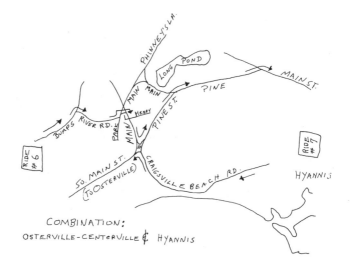

COMBINATION:
OSTERVILLE-CENTERVILLE & HYANNIS

How to get there: See directions on page 22 to Osterville—Centerville or page 26 to Hyannis.

23. Combination: Osterville — Centerville & Hyannis

Number of miles: 27.5
Approximate pedaling time: 4 hours
Terrain: Mostly flat, a few moderate hills
Surface: Good
Things to see: Towns of Osterville, Centerville, and Hyannis; Hyannis Harbor; 1856 Country Store; Centerville Historical Museum; Craigville Beach, and Kalmus Beach Park

This ride combines Ride 6, Osterville—Centerville, with Ride 7, Hyannis. Since the rides overlap for the 0.25-mile section of Centerville's Main Street, if you start in Osterville (page 21), ride all the way around to Centerville's exceptional Main Street. After you have visited the 1856 Country Store and arrived at the traffic light at the intersection of Pine to the left, South Main to the right, and Craigville Beach Road straight ahead, instead of turning right onto South Main, turn left onto Pine Street. In less than a mile Main Street will merge in from the left, and you are now on the Hyannis ride. Follow its directions until you arrive back at the intersection of Craigville Beach Road, Pine, and the two Main streets, whereupon you turn left and get back on the Osterville—Centerville ride, on your way back to the starting place.

If you begin from Hyannis, go the same way once you get to the intersection of Craigville Beach Road, Pine, and the two Main streets, turning left toward Osterville. Do the Osterville—Centerville ride around to its colorful Main Street and then get back onto the Hyannis ride by turning left onto Pine.

If that seems confusing, try reading it again, and be sure to check the map for this combo ride when you come to the place where the rides join.

24. Oak Bluffs — Edgartown (Martha's Vineyard)

Number of miles: 20.5
Approximate pedaling time: $2^1/_2$ hours
Terrain: Flat to moderately hilly
Surface: Fair
Things to see: Joseph Sylvia State Beach, Wesleyan Grove Campground, Windfarm Museum, East Chop, the Flying Horses, Felix Neck Wildlife Sanctuary, Ocean Park

This ride can begin either in Oak Bluffs or in Vineyard Haven. It depends on the time of year and the ferry you take. Before October first you can take a ferry to Vineyard Haven or Oak Bluffs from Wood Hole, Falmouth, or Hyannis; another ferry sails between Nantucket and Oak Bluffs. After October first, however, Vineyard Haven is the only landing.

If you land at Oak Bluffs, begin the ride where you get off the ferry, at the junction of Bluffs Avenue and Seaview Avenue. Go to the right, and, riding up to the end of the point on Seaview, loop around it on Circuit Avenue until you come to Pasque Avenue. Here you will have to turn left, because Circuit suddenly becomes one-way against you. Go up Pasque to Seaview and take a right; turn right again at Bluffs Avenue and follow Bluffs to Circuit. Stop here for a walking tour of Circuit Avenue on the left. Circuit is Oak Bluffs's main street; bikes are not allowed. At the intersection you'll see a carousel called "Flying Horses."

Mount up again, head down Bluffs Avenue, and turn left onto Central Avenue. This little street will take you uphill to the Martha's Vineyard Campmeeting Association. At the top of the hill bear left, then right on Montgomery Avenue to come out at Trinity Park Tabernacle. Turn right and circle around the park. Explore this unique community of narrow streets crowded with ornate, colorful, tiny cottages. After making the circuit, turn right onto Highland Avenue at the foot of Tabernacle Park and then right again onto Siloam Avenue. Siloam joins Duke County Avenue. Bear right and proceed to Lake Avenue. Sunset Lake is on the left.

Turn left onto Lake Avenue, which borders Oak Bluffs Harbor, and then right onto East Chop Drive, which goes alongside the water and then up a short hill. Go up onto the bluff and around the

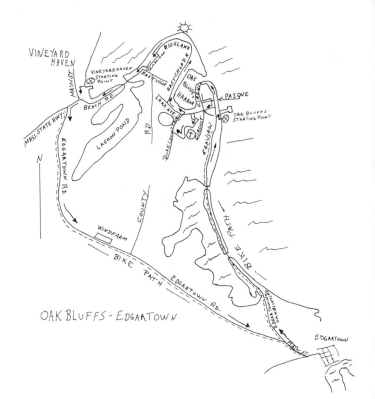

VINEYARD HAVEN

VINEYARD HAVEN STARTING POINT ⊗

MAIN ST.

BEACH RD.

MASS. STATE HWY.

N

EDGARTOWN RD.

LAGOON POND

COUNTY RD.

EAST VILLE

HIGHLAND

EASTCHOP RD.

OAK BLUFFS HARBOR

LAKE AVE.

DUKE COUNTY

CIRCUIT

SEAVIEW

PASQUE

OAK BLUFFS STARTING POINT ⊗

WINDFARM

BIKE PATH

EDGARTOWN RD.

BIKE PATH

OAK BLUFFS

MAIN ST.

EDGARTOWN

OAK BLUFFS - EDGARTOWN

How to get there: Take a ferry to Oak Bluffs or Vineyard Haven and follow the directions in the first section of the ride.

point of land called East Chop on Highland Drive and Atlantic Avenue. You'll pass the East Chop Lighthouse and then enjoy a downhill that yields a fabulous view. Your road goes sharply left soon after this, and then you turn right on Temahigan Avenue, which comes in from the left.

When Temahigan tees into Eastville Avenue, turn right. Eastville may not be marked. If it isn't, use the Martha's Vineyard Hospital, which is across the road in front of you, as a marker. Next, turn almost immediately left onto Beach Road, which takes you alongside the harbor over the causeway to Vineyard Haven. Beach Road follows the contour of the harbor, right then left, past Water Street on the right, to the fork with Main and Edgartown Road. (Note: If you landed at Vineyard Haven, you join the ride at this point. To get here, turn left as soon as you leave the ferry and ride down Main to Beach Road and turn right to Edgartown Road.)

Turn left onto Edgartown Road and ride across to the bike path on the right side of the road. It's a two-way street for bicycles, so keep to the right. This bike path will take you all the way to Edgartown! About 2 miles along the way look for the outdoor, "must see" Windfarm Museum over on the left.

After your visit go back to the bike path and turn left for a 6.5-mile, cars-, truck-, and moped-free ride to Edgartown.

If you like nature walks, there is the Felix Neck Wildlife Sanctuary about 1.5 miles from the County Road intersection on the left. Two miles further you'll come to the outskirts of Edgartown, where Beach Road joins Edgartown Road from the left. There's a sign reading BIKE RTE. CROSSING. Continue on into Edgartown if you want to explore the town, but if you are ready to go back to Oak Bluffs or Vineyard Haven, turn sharply left and north to start the bike trail, *another* paved bike path that parallels Beach Road and the water for the 5-mile trip to Oak Bluffs. You'll soon see Segekontacket Pond on your left and the beach for Edgartown residents on your right. The beach on the other side of the bridge over the inlet to Segekontacket Pond is Sylvia State Beach, where you can swim, fish, and/or picnic. Continue north toward Oak Bluffs. The bike path ends at Seaview Avenue, so ride along Seaview to the Oak Bluffs ferry landing.

To get back to Vineyard Haven, follow the directions to Eastville Road and then retrace your route to Vineyard Haven.

25. Chappaquiddick (Martha's Vineyard)

Number of miles: 7.5
Approximate pedaling time: 1 hour
Terrain: Flat to rolling
Surface: Fair
Things to see: East Beach, Cape Poge Light, Wasque Wildlife Preservation Area, Dike Bridge, On Time ferry

Get on the tiny On Time ferry from Edgartown to Chappaquiddick, which plies its brief route continually from 7:30 a.m. until midnight during the season (and until 6:00 p.m. in the off-season). The one-way fares, as of July 1990, are: bike and rider—$2.50; car and driver—$4.00; passengers—$1.00; motorcycle or moped and rider—$3.50; horses and cattle—75 cents; freight—$1.50 per ton. The passage takes only a *minute*, so savor every *second* of the view of Edgartown, with its elegant captains' houses and lighthouse, and of Edgartown Harbor, dotted with boats of all kinds. To your right is Katama Bay. Debark onto Chappaquiddick and proceed straight ahead; there will be many bicycles, and they are instructed to KEEP RIGHT. RIDE SINGLE FILE. You'll go by a beach club on the left and Caleb's Inlet on the right. The route goes up an incline. Be sure to pause at the top for the view of Edgartown and its environs. At about the 2-mile point, Chappaquiddick Road curves sharply right ninety degrees. Straight ahead is an unpaved dirt/sand road. This is Dike Road. Take it and it will lead you to the famous Dike Bridge (now a part of American history), East Beach, and Cape Poge. East Beach, about 3 miles from the ferry landing, is part of the Cape Poge Wildlife Preserve and is a beautiful white sand beach on the Atlantic. A long neck, Cape Poge, extends to the north. Trek out there for privacy, dunes exploration, and to see the lighthouse and views of Martha's Vineyard. This sand bar protects Cape Poge Bay, as it curves around in an elbow shape. Camping on these beaches is not allowed, but you can spend day after day out here experiencing the sun and the sand (and the mystery of the Chappaquiddick Dike Bridge). When you leave the beach, retrace your route up the dirt road, past the two houses and the Toms Neck Farm Pre-serve on the right, which is a commercial shooting range.

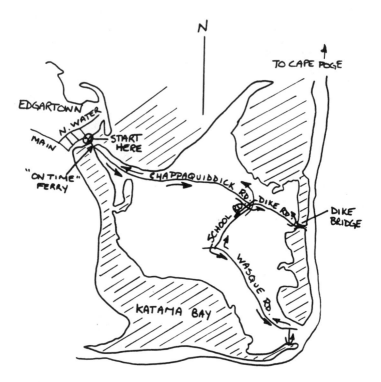

N

TO CAPE POGE

EDGARTOWN

N. WATER

MAIN

START HERE

"ON TIME" FERRY

CHAPPAQUIDDICK RD.

DIKE RD.

DIKE BRIDGE

SCHOOL

WASQUE RD.

KATAMA BAY

CHAPPAQUIDDICK

How to get there: Go to the wharf at the end of Main Street in Edgartown, park, and ride to the Town Dock, which is at the foot of Daggett Street.

When you come to paved Chappaquiddick Road again, turn left. Here the road is also called School Road. Take it to a T intersection with Wasque Road on the left (paved) and Litchfield Road on the right (unpaved). Turn left onto Wasque Road. It soon becomes a dirt/sand road, so you have to ride carefully. Like many roads on Martha's Vineyard, Wasque Road has many private roads leading from it. Continue to Wasque Point, where the 150-acre Wasque Reservation is open to the public. When you come to a fork and one-way signs, take the road that goes right ninety degrees to the beach. Return to the School Road junction after exploring Wasque Point and turn right and ride back to the On Time ferry.

26. Edgartown — Katama (South) Beach
(Martha's Vineyard)

Number of miles: 10.5
Approximate pedaling time: 1 $\frac{1}{4}$ hours
Terrain: Flat to moderately hilly
Surface: Fair
Things to see: Numerous captains' houses, Thomas Cooke House Museum, First Federated Church, Edgartown Lighthouse, On Time ferry, Sheriff's Meadow, Katama (South) Beach

This ride tours Edgartown and then loops down to Katama Beach and back. It starts at the Town Dock in Edgartown. Go along Dock Street the brief distance between Main and Daggett to the On Time ferry landing and the Public Wharf. Go up to the observation deck of the wharf for views of Edgartown, the harbor, and Chappaquiddick Island, and then ride up Daggett Street to North Water Street. (If Daggett is one-way you can walk your bike this short distance.) To your right is the Daggett House Inn built in 1750 and open to the public. Turn right. From here to the end of the street are Martha's Vineyard's handsomest captains' houses. Several were built at an angle to afford views of homebound ships rounding Cape Poge. The chimneys, picket fences, door fans, and other well-crafted wood details contribute to the elegance of these houses, built in the early nineteenth century. The bike route takes you past some but not all of these, so do some additional touring of stately Edgartown if you have time.

At the end of North Water Street, lock up your bike and walk to the lighthouse, and then turn left onto Starbuck Neck Road. Starbuck Neck Road comes to a T at Fuller Street. Turn left here and head back toward Main Street.

At Morse Street turn right and then immediately left on North Summer Street. On this street pass the little red brick St. Andrew's Church, the Christine Pease House, and the Captain Henry Holt House (1828), now a guest house.

On Main Street turn left, go one block, and then turn right on South Water Street. Here you'll pass several old, handsome white frame houses with bright green shutters, all of them of historic interest. Proceed on South Water Street. You'll soon see

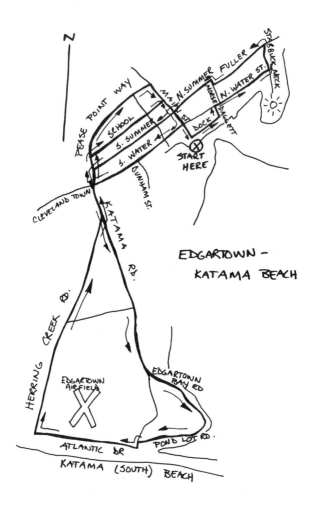

EDGARTOWN –
KATAMA BEACH

How to get there: Take the Edgartown Road from Vineyard Haven or Oak Bluffs or the West Tisbury Road from the direction of Gay Head. Take Main Street to the Town Dock.

Dunham Street going off to your left; go down Dunham to explore that area if you like; otherwise, proceed to where South Water meets Cleveland Town Road and Katama Road and turn right. Go uphill to School Street and turn right. On the corner of School and Cooke streets, visit the Thomas Cooke House Museum and then ride back to Main Street. (Edgartown's one-way streets require lacing back and forth in this manner.)

At Main Street turn right in front of the courthouse. At South Summer Street turn right again. Enjoy the diversity of the shops on Main Street and South Summer Street. South Summer Street has many historically significant buildings, including the First Federated Church (1828).

When you return to Pease Point Way, turn left and head south to Katama Beach, on Katama Road. Take the bike path on the left side of Katama Road. Bear left at the fork with Edgartown Bay Road. At the fork with Town Lot Road, remain on Edgartown Bay Road. Circle around the point. The barrier beach can be seen from here. Proceed west to rejoin Katama Road. Turn left heading toward Katama Beach. Your road tees into Atlantic Drive, which parallels Mattakesset Herring Creek. Katama Beach is a beautiful 3-mile-long white sand beach. There is surf on the ocean side of the barrier and salt water pond swimming on the bay side.

When you're ready to leave the area, go west on Atlantic Drive. Turn right on Herring Creek Road, ride past the air field and Crocker Road, and rejoin Katama Road.

When you cross South Water Street, the road becomes Pease Point Way once more. Take it to Main Street. At the junction with Main Street you may turn right, going past the Dr. Daniel Fisher House and the Methodist Church, to end your ride at the Town Dock at the foot of Main Street; or, if you would enjoy a side trip to a nature sanctuary, cross Main Street and continue north. Here, Pease Point Way is called Planting Field Way, and it will take you directly to Sheriff's Meadow. This eighteen-acre wildlife preserve has foot trails through woods and marshlands, including a 6-mile loop around Eel Pond with Vineyard Sound as a backdrop. After your visit retrace your route to Main Street and turn left to reach the Town Dock.

27. Vineyard Haven—Lambert's Cove
(Martha's Vineyard)

Number of miles: 15.5
Approximate pedaling time: 2 hours
Terrain: Hilly
Surface: Good
Things to see: Vineyard Haven, West Chop, Lambert's Cove Road, Seamen's Bethel, Williams Street houses, Cedar Tree Neck

Start this ride at the ferry landing in Vineyard Haven. If you had to bring your car, park it in the town parking lot across from the Steamship Authority lot. Since the island is small and parking is scarce, it would be better to leave your car at Woods Hole and just bring yourself and your bike.

Facing away from the dock, turn left on Water Street and then right on Beach Street, and then go uphill the short distance to Main, where you turn right. Main Street now goes uphill toward West Chop. As you climb, you can take in all of beautiful Vineyard Haven Harbor. The hill soon crests and you start a downhill run of nearly a half mile. At the bottom of the hill, Main Street changes its name to West Chop Avenue.

As you go out on the West Chop bluffs the houses get larger. One mile farther on West Chop Avenue, which rolls up and down, you'll notice a BIKE ROUTE sign on the left side of the road. At the top of West Chop, there's an overlook of the ocean, complete with flagpole and bench. The bike route, which you follow, makes a loop to the left through West Chop woods. At the point where Franklin Street comes in from the right, you continue straight ahead, following the BIKE ROUTE sign. Within a short distance you will have completed the loop and will be back at West Chop Avenue, where you turn right.

Come back on West Chop Avenue to Woodlawn Avenue, the next street after the public library. You must turn right here because Main Street is one-way against you at this point. From Woodlawn turn left on Franklin Street. Ride to Spring Street and turn left. Go one block and turn right one hundred thirty-five degrees onto William. The WILLIAM street sign is on the corner to your left. Curve uphill to the right and stay on William until it tees with Pine Tree

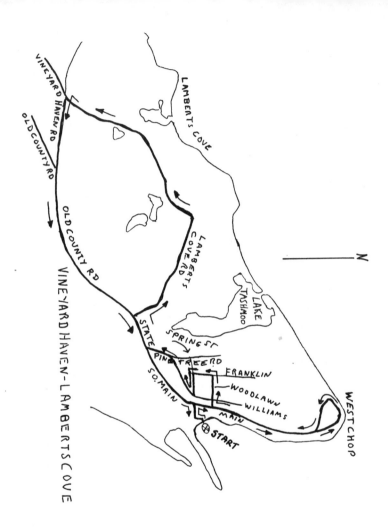

N

VINEYARD HAVEN RD
OLD COUNTY RD
OLD COUNTY RD
VINEYARD HAVEN-LAMBERTS COVE
LAMBERTS COVE
LAMBERTS COVE RD
LAKE TASHMOO
SPRING ST
STATE RD
PINE TREE RD
SO. MAIN
FRANKLIN
WOODLAWN
WILLIAMS
MAIN
WEST CHOP
START

How to get there: Take the ferry from Woods Hole to Vineyard Haven. If you take one of the ferries to Oak Bluffs, follow the signs to Vineyard Haven.

Road. Turn left. Pine Tree soon comes to a T at State Road at an angle, where you turn right, heading west, downhill on curving, rolling State Road.

In 0.6 mile you come to a turnout on the right with a magnificent view of Lake Tashmoo and the Elizabeth Islands over rolling hills. In less than a half mile you should see a sign for LAMBERT'S COVE. Turn right at the sign, onto Lambert's Cove Road. If the sign is missing, there should at least be a sign on the left side reading: GAYHEAD 17 VINEYARD HAVEN 2. You're now in horse country, with old farms and stone walls and a patch of forest now and again. One mile from the turn onto Lambert's Cove Road, start a nice downhill run. Just before this hill is the entrance to Cranberry Acres, one of three privately owned campgrounds open to the public.

In 0.5 mile you pass into West Tisbury and go abruptly uphill, and then around a curve and down again. This is a hilly road but very scenic with views of forests and open, flat areas on either side. Pass Duarte Pond on the left and then an old country cemetery on the right. In another 0.4 mile, start a brief but steep uphill climb to beautiful little Lambert's Cove Methodist Church. Lambert's Cove Road curves around to the left, past Seth's Pond and up a 0.4-mile-long grade to the intersection with Vineyard Haven Road. Take a sharp left turn onto Vineyard Haven Road heading back toward Vineyard Haven.

If you like to walk along nature trails, take a side trip here by turning right instead of left, going a short distance, and turning forty-five degrees right onto Indian Hill Road. Follow this road for 0.75 mile to the end. Just before the turnaround, a sign on the right directs you to Vineyard Sound. Take this dirt road 1 mile to the Cedar Tree Neck Wildlife Sanctuary. No swimming or picnicking is permitted, but communing is encouraged.

Continue the ride on Vineyard Haven Road. Soon Old County Road comes in from the right and merges with Vineyard Haven Road. Bear left and continue on this well-paved road, which is now taking you through flat countryside. About 1.5 miles from this point pass Lambert's Cove Road on the left and continue on into Vineyard Haven as Old County Road changes to State Road and then to South Main Street as it curves downward into town. Continue past Main Street to Water Street and turn left to end up where you started.

28. West Tisbury — Menemsha (Martha's Vineyard)

Number of miles: 16
Approximate pedaling time: 2 hours
Terrain: Definitely hilly and curving
Surface: Fair
Things to see: Menemsha Harbor, village of West Tisbury, Chilmark Center, seascapes

If you have come to the Vineyard without an automobile, you can begin this ride in North Tisbury at the Y intersection of Vineyard Haven Road, North Road, and South Road.

If you have an automobile, you can go down the left fork, South Road, about 1.5 miles to West Tisbury and park near the General Store and Post Office. Once on your bike, ride back up to the Y and turn left onto North Road, following the arrow that points the way to Menemsha. You're on a lovely curving road that goes through wooded areas of trees and thickets but also provides some views of walled pasture land and of Vineyard Sound. About 3 miles from the fork you will pass Tea Lane, a tree-lined, narrow, dirt road, to your left. This section of road continues to be quite hilly. About 2 miles from Tea Lane, the road crests, providing a vista of Menemsha Pond. Soon you will go sharply downhill, past the sign to Gay Head and Chilmark, into the tiny fishing hamlet of Menemsha; there are several docks, fishing shacks clinging to the littoral, small boats, and large fishing vessels. You'll also spot boats for charter and a fine anchorage for visiting pleasure craft. After you go out on the dirt road alongside the inlet to Menemsha Pond, come back and turn left at the first paved road and go out to Dutcher's Dock, passing a couple of art galleries, stopping for a snack and a look at the village fish markets where everything from lobster to eels may be purchased fresh daily, and proceeding on to the little public beach.

When you're ready, return to North Road and go up the steep hill to the intersection with Menemsha Cross Road, which may not be so marked but should have a sign GAY HEAD-CHILMARK. Turn right and proceed about 1 mile to Beetlebung Corner with its handsome Methodist Church and fire and police stations.

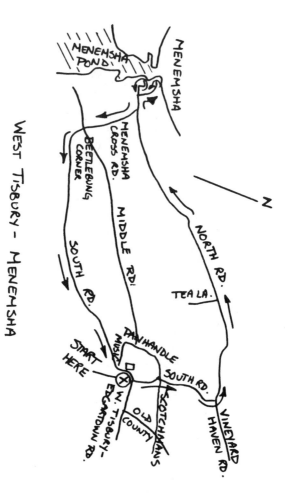

WEST TISBURY – MENEMSHA

How to get there: Refer to the first section of the ride itself.

Beetlebung is the old Islander name for the tupelo trees you'll see here, and the "Corner" is the intersection of Menemsha Cross Road, Middle Road to your left, and South Road, which is both to your right and straight ahead.

You go straight ahead on South Road, which turns sharply left in a few hundred yards to begin the eastward leg toward West Tisbury. All along this portion of the ride are views of ponds, hills, the ocean, and the stone walls of old sheep farms; it is also hilly, and, combined with the up-island's typical narrow, curvy roads, it spells caution.

In about 3 miles, a long downhill run offers an expansive view of moors, dunes, and ocean. This will be followed by a gradual uphill grade before you arrive in the village of West Tisbury in about 2 miles. Here you'll find a grange, Congregational church on the left, art gallery (with Picassoesque sculptures in the garden) on the right, and fine old white frame houses.

Sir Joshua Slocum, who was the first to circumnavigate the globe alone in his motorless sloop *Spray*, made his home here for many years before being lost at sea in 1907. His house can be reached by taking a short detour up South Road and then right onto Edgartown—West Tisbury Road. The house is on the right.

Alley's General Store in West Tisbury is well worth a visit. You can get an apple or candy bar before loading bike on car—if that's the way you came—or continuing up South Road, past the intersection with Edgartown–West Tisbury Road. Soon there'll be a sharp left—with a cemetery straight ahead for those who came to Martha's Vineyard and never left. You will cross Mill Brook and soon be back at the Y with North Road and Vineyard Haven Road.

29. Gay Head (Martha's Vineyard)

Number of miles: 11.2
Approximate pedaling time: $1^1/_2$ hours
Terrain: Definitely hilly and curving
Surface: Fair
Things to see: Gay Head Cliffs and Lighthouse, Menemsha Pond, Elizabeth Islands

Start your ride at the mile-long Gay Head Cliffs at Martha's Vineyard's westernmost tip, about 19 miles from Vineyard Haven. There are public facilities located at this National Historic Landmark, as well as snack bars and souvenir shops. These glacial cliffs, millions of years old, are made of multi-layered clays of different colors. Paleontologists have uncovered bones of ancient whales, horses, and camels in the area. One couldn't tire of the views afforded from this site: the cliffs themselves, whose clays color the water crashing into them; the western seascape of the lighthouse; the Chilmark hills; and the ponds, dunes, and beaches of Martha's Vineyard.

When you leave the cliffs, bear left on the one-way loop and then turn right on Moshup Trail. Head downhill toward the water. The Gay Head Town Beach is on the right. Summer houses are perched randomly among the hills and dunes, and the dunes are covered with grasses like bear's fur. Low shrubs, bushes, and stunted trees provide the vegetation at Gay Head. The effect is rather desolate but also unique and therefore arresting. Moshup Trail parallels the coast. About a mile from the cliffs Old South Road enters from the left. About 2 miles after this junction a long grade of about 0.7 mile begins. Stop occasionally for resting and viewing Zachs Cliffs, Long Beach, Squibnocket Pond, and other sights.

At South Road, where there's a stop sign but maybe not a street sign, turn left. The road soon crests and then continues its up and down formations, continuing to snake around as well. At the sign LOBSTERVILLE TOWN BEACH turn right onto Lobsterville Road (there once was a fishing community here by this name). Enjoy a great downhill ride here as you head toward Vineyard Sound. In a little over a mile, Lighthouse Road joins you from the left, but you continue straight ahead and then bear left on West Basin Road.

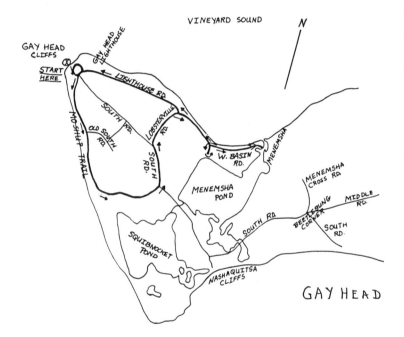

VINEYARD SOUND

N

GAY HEAD
CLIFFS

START
HERE

GAY HEAD LIGHTHOUSE

LIGHTHOUSE RD.

SOUTH RD.

OLD SOUTH RD.

MOSHUP TRAIL

LOBSTERVILLE RD.

SOUTH RD.

W. BASIN RD.

MENEMSHA

MENEMSHA POND

MENEMSHA CROSS RD.

BEETLEBUNG CORNER

MIDDLE RD.

SOUTH RD.

SOUTH RD.

SQUIBNOCKET POND

NASHAQUITSA CLIFFS

GAY HEAD

How to get there: From Vineyard Haven or elsewhere on the island, go west on major roads following signs to Gay Head.

Follow this road to its end, with Vineyard Sound on your left and Menemsha Pond on your right. An Adriatic-like pebbly beach is all along this road amid sand dunes. Directly ahead at the end of the road is Menemsha Bight, an inlet of the sound.

You face the village of Menemsha across the bight, but you can't get there from here. (Visit the hamlet on the West Tisbury—Menemsha ride.) Menemsha's harbor is beautifully protected and so is full of fishing and pleasure craft year-round.

Turn around and head back up West Basin Road. Take a brief detour down to the pond's edge and the public landing when you come upon a road going off to the left. Return to West Basin Road and proceed straight ahead to its intersection with Lobsterville and Lighthouse Road. Turn right and head west on Lighthouse Road. Summer houses also dot the terrain on this side of Gay Head. After about 2 miles on Lighthouse Road you'll arrive at the Gay Head Lighthouse, built in 1952. The first lighthouse on this site was built in 1799. Continue to the Gay Head Cliffs and the end of the ride.

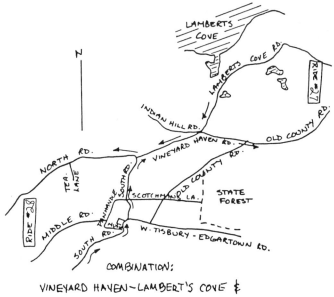

COMBINATION:

VINEYARD HAVEN~LAMBERT'S COVE &
WEST TISBURY~MENEMSHA

How to get there: Take the ferry from Woods Hole to Vineyard Haven. If you take one of the ferries to Oak Bluffs, follow the signs to Vineyard Haven.

30. Combination: Vineyard Haven — Lambert's Cove & West Tisbury — Menemsha
(Martha's Vineyard)

Number of miles: 35
Approximate pedaling time: $4^1/_2$ hours
Terrain: Hilly
Surface: Good
Things to see: Vineyard Haven, West Chop, Lambert's Cove Road, Seamen's Bethel, Williams Street houses, Cedar Tree Neck, Menemsha Harbor, village of West Tisbury, Chilmark Center, seascapes

The six rides on Martha's Vineyard cover most of the island and can be ridden one at a time or in combinations, depending on such things as the time of year—days are longer in summer, whether you came by car or bike alone, whether you've come for the day or a longer stay, where you are staying, and, when all's been said and done, how well you feel.

If you're game, try putting rides 27 and 28 together by starting out from Vineyard Haven on the Vineyard Haven—Lambert's Cove ride; when you get to the point where Lambert's Cove Road meets Vineyard Haven Road, go right instead of left onto the latter and ride about 1.5 miles to the Y with South and North roads. Turn right onto North Road and make the complete 16-mile circuit of the West Tisbury—Menemsha ride (28).

When you arrive back at the Y with South and North roads, bear right and go back the 1.5 miles to the junction of Vineyard Haven and Lambert's Cove roads, bear to the right, and do the last half of the Vineyard Haven—Lambert's Cove ride, back into Vineyard Haven.

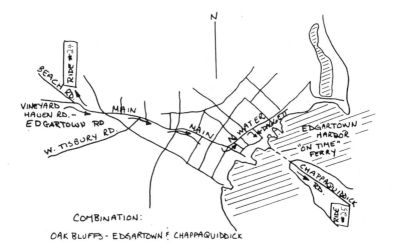

N

COMBINATION:
OAK BLUFFS - EDGARTOWN & CHAPPAQUIDDICK

How to get there: Take a ferry to Oak Bluffs or Vineyard Haven and follow the directions in the first section of ride 24.

31. Combination: Oak Bluffs—Edgartown & Chappaquiddick (Martha's Vineyard)

Number of miles: 28
Approximate pedaling time: 4 hours
Terrain: Flat to moderately hilly
Surface: Fair
Things to see: Joseph Sylvia State Beach, Wesleyan Grove Campground, Windfarm Museum, East Chop, the Flying Horses, Felix Neck Wildlife Sanctuary, Ocean Park, East Beach, Cape Poge Light, Wasque Wildlife Preservation Area, Dike Bridge, On Time ferry

This combination ride will start out in either Oak Bluffs or Vineyard Haven and follow the route of the Oak Bluffs—Edgartown ride (ride 24) to the point where Beach Road joins Edgartown Road, a short distance from the center of Edgartown. Instead of turning sharply left, continue straight into Edgartown. You'll be on Main Street. Follow it and the signs to the CHAPPY FERRY down to North Water Street; turn left to Daggett, turn right, and you will see the tiny little three-car ferry. It's called the On Time ferry because, not having a schedule, it's always on time.

Now you are at the beginning of the Chappaquiddick ride (ride 25). When you come back on the ferry, make your way back to the junction of Edgartown—Vineyard Haven Road and Beach Road, which is also called the Edgartown—Oak Bluffs Road; bear right and continue the Oak Bluffs—Edgartown ride on the bike path along the ocean to Oak Bluffs.

32. Nantucket Town—Surfside (Nantucket)

Number of miles: 10.2
Approximate pedaling time: 2 hours
Terrain: Flat to moderately hilly
Surface: Good to excellent
Things to see: The marvelous town of Nantucket itself, the Peter Foulger Museum, the Whaling Museum, Surfside Beach

Start at Steamboat Wharf where the ferry comes in. There are two bike shops here in case you need supplies or repairs or want to rent a bike. Go up Broad Street past Easy Street (which is one-way coming from your left). Ride past Beach Street, the Peter Foulger Museum, and the Whaling Museum.

Turn left on South Water Street and then right on Main Street. Main is paved with small, irregular cobblestones dating from the 1830s. These stones had served as ballast; they were laid to prevent wagons laden with oil casks from sinking into the sand. They were a boon in the 1800s, but they are a bane to cyclists today.

Go up Main Street to the bank and bear left. Where Gardner comes in from the right, Main Street goes right forty-five degrees, but you bear left on Milk Street, passing Vestal on the right. At the fork, bear left on New Mill, which is one-way against you, so walk your bike. The next street is Prospect; turn left. Watch for street signs. (Since the houses are built close together, down to the edge of the narrow sidewalks, the street signs are often hung on the sides of the houses.)

At the fork, bear right onto South Prospect Street and go about 0.25 mile to the intersection of Prospect, Williams, Sparks, and Atlantic Avenue (also called Surfside Road). The sign says HOSPITAL and SURFSIDE. Turn almost ninety degrees right onto Atlantic. Within a short distance, across from the Nantucket High School, you will find a bike path on the right side of Atlantic Avenue. Cross over it and enjoy a 2.5-mile ride to the beach, one of the island's most popular, with lifeguard, snack bar, and bathhouse.

After a surfeit of sun and surf, return along the same route to the Old Mill on the corner of South Prospect, York, and South Mill streets.

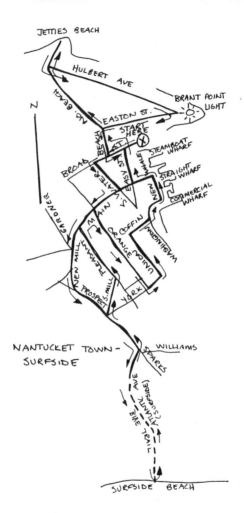

JETTIES BEACH

HULBERT AVE

BRANT POINT LIGHT

NO. BEACH

EASTON ST.

N

START HERE

STEAMBOAT WHARF

BROAD

BEACH ST.

EASY ST.

WHALE

STRAIGHT WHARF

S. WATER

NEW

COMMERCIAL WHARF

GARDNER

MAIN

OR COFFIN

UNION

WASHINGTON

NEW MILL

PLEASANT

S. MILL

YORK

PROSPECT

NANTUCKET TOWN - SURFSIDE

WILLIAMS

SPARKS

ATLANTIC (SURFSIDE)

AVE

BIKE TRAIL

SURFSIDE BEACH

How to get there: Take the Nantucket ferry from Woods Hole or Hyannis to Nantucket Town.

Turn right around the site of the Old Mill onto South Mill Street with the mill on your left. This is the one survivor of the four that originally stood on the hill, grinding corn. Go downhill on South Mill Street. Turn left at the bottom of the hill at the T intersection with Pleasant Street. Proceed along Pleasant Street to Main, where you turn right. On the corner, at 96 Main Street, is the Hawden-Satler House. The three Georgian brick mansions across the street are identical. They were built between 1836 and 1838 by William Starbuck, a whaler, for his three sons. The middle house is still inhabited by descendants of the original owner. A Starbuck whaling ship set two records in 1859: It returned with 6,000 barrels of oil after a five-year voyage!

At Orange Street turn right. There may not be a sign for Orange Street, but there will be a series of signposts reading: SURFSIDE-BIKE PATH; POLPIS-WAUWINET; HOSPITAL-AIRPORT, AND SIASCONSET BIKEPATH. More houses of whaling ship captains line Orange Street than any other street in the world. Go to York Street, turn left and left again onto Union Street, and head back toward the center of town. At Coffin Street turn right and go to Washington. Turn left and then immediately right and head toward Commercial (Swain's) Wharf.

Lock your bike to any handy post here and walk around the three public wharves: Commercial, Straight, and Old South. Commercial fishing and scalloping boats still come and go.

From here proceed around the parking area on New Whale Street, turn up Main, and then go along Easy Street four short blocks to Broad. If you have time for a swim, turn left on Broad and then right onto South Beach Street. Go three blocks to the stop sign at Easton Street. Jog across to North Beach Street. Head up a slight hill. Beyond the Bird Sanctuary on the left, bear right where the sign says JETTIES BEACH, the main public beach on the island. There is a gently sloping beach on one side and a shallow beach for children on the other. There is a lifeguard, bathhouse, and restaurant.

Leaving Jetties Beach, take the first left, Hulbert Avenue. Follow it to Brant Point Light. Go right out to the point. Come back and continue straight ahead on Easton to the intersection with North and South Beach streets. Turn left onto South Beach and proceed back to Steamboat Wharf.

33. Madaket   (Nantucket)

Number of miles: 15.7
Approximate pedaling time: 2 hours
Terrain: Flat to gently rolling
Surface: Very good. Bike path for most of the route
Things to see: The western end of Nantucket with its moors, Dionis Beach, Madaket Harbor and Beach, Hither Creek, Eel Point

Start this ride in front of the Peter Foulger Museum on Broad Street. Turn left on South Water Street to Main Street. Turn right and continue up cobbled Main, which becomes Madaket Road. In short order you will come to Canton Circle with a flagpole in the center where Main, Lowell Place, Quaker, and Madaket roads meet. On the left side there is a great bike path that runs all the way to Madaket, a distance of approximately 5 miles.

About 1.5 miles from Canton Circle you'll reach Eel Point Road and a sign saying DIONIS BEACH. If you are in the mood for beautiful sand dunes, a lifeguard, rest rooms, and gentle surf, turn right. The beach is down the road about 0.75 mile. When you are ready, come back to the Madaket Road bike path and continue across the heath—or moor as the islanders call it—toward the western end of the island.

In about 2 miles you'll cross over an inlet between the two halves of Long Pond, and then the road and path turn left and go straight to Madaket Beach, which is on the Atlantic side and is another splendid beach.

When you come back from the beach, turn left and go across the little bridge over the westernmost end of Hither Creek to Smith Point on the left or Jackson Point on the right and then come back to Madaket Road and turn back to the left. When you come to a sign that reads HITHER CREEK BOATYARD or CAMBRIDGE STREET, turn left. This will take you to Little Neck, a Nantucket Conservation Foundation property open to the public.

If you have time, you can also turn left when you reach Warren's Landing Road and take this dirt road out 1.5 miles to Eel Point, a 128-acre wildlife reservation. Coming back to Madaket Road and the bike path, turn left once more and take a leisurely ride all the way back to Main Street and Nantucket Town.

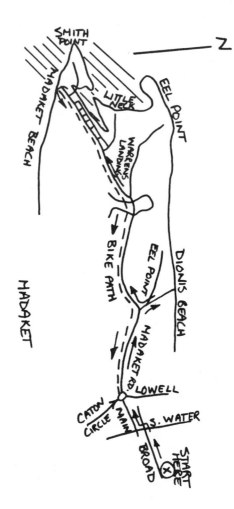

How to get there: Take the Nantucket ferry from Woods Hole or Hyannis to Nantucket Town.

34. Siasconset (Nantucket)

Number of miles: 26.0 or 22.5
Approximate pedaling time: $2^3/_4$ hours
Terrain: Flat to moderately hilly
Surface: Good to poor
Things to see: Nantucket Harbor, Wauwinet, Sankaty Head Light, Siasconset, Siasconset Beach

Start this ride at the foot of Main Street in front of the Pacific Club. In 1859, a group of former whaling ship captains who had sailed the Pacific formed the club for "yarning" together.

Walk up the square (because of the cobblestones); just before reaching the Pacific National Bank, turn left onto Orange Street. There may not be an ORANGE STREET sign, but there will be a series of signposts reading: SURFSIDE-BIKE PATH; POLPIS-WAUWINET; HOSPITAL-AIRPORT, and SIASCONSET BIKE PATH. The latter is the destination for which you are heading. About 1 mile from the start, you will come to the Milestone Rotary identified by a sign: POLPIS SIASCONSET. Go around to the left and onto the Milestone Bike Path, which starts here. This path will take you straight down to the only other town on Nantucket, Siasconset, called Sconset for short. The bike path is 6 miles long, most of it gently downhill.

You are now getting your first look at Nantucket's open heath or moor with its great variety of wildflowers, bayberry, scrub oaks, pine groves, and purple scotch heather. The first settlers found a treeless island. The Coffin brothers imported 30,000 pine trees in 1851 and planted them in these outlying areas. About 0.5 mile after the bike path ends you will come to a rotary that is distinguished by a flagpole made from a ship's spar. Here you go around to the right, uphill on Ocean Avenue, also called Beach Road, which goes along a bluff overlooking the Atlantic Ocean. On the right side are Nantucket's larger summer homes. The view to the left is spectacular! You can ride out as far as the Coast Guard Loran Station before turning around, or you can turn around whenever you like and come back. Just before the rotary take a hairpin turn downhill and around to the right under the footbridge to Sconset Beach. There are bike racks and miles of beach stretching in either direction.

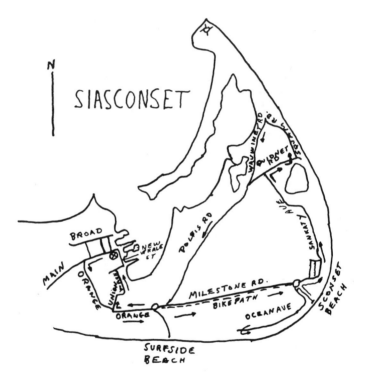

N

SIASCONSET

BROAD
NEW WHALE ST
MAIN
ORANGE
UNION ST
ORANGE
POLPIS RD
MADAKET RD
QUIDNET RD
QUIDNET
SANKATY
SCONSET BEACH
MILESTONE RD.
BIKE PATH
OCEAN AVE
SURFSIDE BEACH

How to get there: Take the Nantucket ferry from Woods Hole or Hyannis to Nantucket Town.

When you have picnicked or just rested, come back under the footbridge to the rotary, where you turn right and go into the town of Sconset with its doll-sized cottages. Originally fishing shacks, they were enlarged to their present size in the eighteenth century when the women of the fishermen decided to join them. Turn left on Broadway to the Y with Sankaty Road; turn right, heading north. Continue on Sankaty for about 2.5 miles, past Sesachacha Pond on the right, until it tees into Quidnet Road. Turn right onto Quidnet. (If you're getting tired or hungry—or both—you can cut 3.5 miles off the ride by continuing left on Sankaty Road.) In just about a mile you will come to a stop sign and a sandy unpaved road coming in from the left. There is a sign on the left that reads, This is AN ABUTTER'S ROAD. PROCEED AT YOUR OWN RISK. This is Squam Road. Turn left; ride 2 miles on this narrow dirt/sand road, with the ocean on your right and Squam swamp on your left. It's a bit tricky on high-pressure, narrow-width tires, but it is navigable. A mountain bike would take it in stride.

Squam Road ends at Wauwinet Road, where you turn left and roll up and down it until it joins Polpis Road at a Y intersection. Bear right onto Polpis and ride through the moors for 4.5 miles until you come to Milestone Road. Cross over to the other side of Milestone to ride up to the rotary on the bike path. At the rotary turn right onto Orange Street. When you get to Union Street, turn right and follow it around to Francis Street. Turn right and then left onto Washington, which skirts South Beach.

At the point where Washington bears left at the fork with Candle Street, Washington becomes one-way against you. Turn right ninety degrees onto Commercial (or Swain's) Wharf just before the fork and then left on New Whale to tour the wharf area before ending your ride.

Bike Rental Centers

Cape Cod

All Cape Sales, 627 Main Street, West Yarmouth, MA (508) 771-8100
Arnold's, 329 Commercial Street, Provincetown, MA (508) 487-0844
Art's Bike Shop, 75 Country Road, North Falmouth, MA (508) 563-7379
Bill's Bike Shop, 847 E. Main Street, Falmouth, MA (508) 548-7979
Black Duck Sports Shop, Main Street, South Wellfleet, MA (508) 349-9801
Brewster Bicycle Rental, 414 Underpass Road, Brewster, MA
　　　(508) 896-8149
Corner Cycle, 39 North Main Street, Falmouth, MA (508) 540-4195
Cove Cycles, 223 Barnstable Road, Hyannis, MA (508) 771-6155
Doctor Gravity's Kite Shop, 564 Route 28,Harwichport, MA (508) 430-0437
Full Cycle, 7 Merchant Square, Sandwich, MA (508) 888-8445
Idle Times Bike Shop, Nickerson State Park, Route 6A, Brewster, MA
　　　(508) 896-9242
Idle Times Bike Shop, Route 6, Brewster, MA (508) 255-8281
Little Capistrano Bike Shop, Salt Pond Road, Eastam, MA (508) 255-6515
The Outdoor Shop, 50 Long Pond Drive, South Yarmouth, MA
　　　(508) 394-3819

Martha's Vineyard

The Bike Rack, 17 Water Street, Vineyard Haven, MA (508) 693-9031
Cycle Works, State Road, Vineyard Haven, MA (508) 693-6966
R.W. Cutler, Main Street, Edgartown, MA (508) 627-4052

Nantucket

Cook's Cycle Shop, 6 South Beach Street, Nantucket, MA
　　　(508) 228 0800
Fun Rentals, South Beach Street, Nantucket, MA (508) 228-4049
Holiday Cycle,4 Chester, Nantucket, MA (508) 228-3644
Holiday Cycle, 135 Old South Road, Nantucket, MA (508) 228-1525
Nantucket Bike Shop, Steamboat Wharf, Nantucket, MA (508) 228-1999
Young's Bicycle Shop, Steamboat Wharf, Nantucket, MA
　　　(508) 228-1151 (year round)